I Learned
It First in
Sunday School

Dear Ss. Sheur + Bro. Charles

May this book be a blessing to you!
We are so blessed to have you in
the ministry!

w/ love + prayers,

Ss. Maribeth + Bro Ronald + Keda

I Learned It First in Sunday School

Cliff Schimmels

formerly titled
All I Really Need to Know
I Learned in Sunday School

VICTOR BOOKS

A DIVISION OF SCRIPTURE PRESS PUBLICATIONS INC.
USA CANADA ENGLAND

Library of Congress Cataloging-in-Publication Data

Schimmels, Cliff.

   I learned it first in Sunday School / Cliff Schimmels.

      p.   cm.

   ISBN 1-56476-007-3

   1. Sunday schools. I. Title.

BV1521.S35 1991

268 – dc20   91-15460

                                            CIP

2 3 4 5 6 7 8 9 10 Printing/Year 96 95 94 93 92

CONTENTS

DEDICATION

The little girl who sat on her grandma's lap brought laughter to her life.

"Grandma, in Sunday School I learned that Jesus lives in my heart." And then she showed her grandma where, with her little hand pressed firmly.

"That's good," the grandma said, "but how do you know that?"

The little girl pressed even more firmly and exclaimed, "I can feel Him jump!"

A child's understanding, a child's feelings, and a child's precious soul! That's the stuff of Sunday School.

We talk of institutions and programs, of curriculum and structure. We talk of class roles and growth trends, of evangelism and outreach. But we remember the people.

The names you remember are different than mine. The events and settings vary; yet, our memories are a great deal alike because the people have so much in common . . . the teacher who stayed up late at night and made lessons from homemade materials; the kid sitting beside me who got his tongue twisted and brought new insight to a familiar passage; the leader who taught you to sing the song that leaps up still in your mind and mouth at the most unusual times — these are Sunday School.

And to those teachers and leaders and kids in my memories and yours, to the parents who dressed us and got us there and then quizzed us when we got home, to the little girl with Jesus jumping in her heart, and to the teacher who taught her almost that, I offer my thanks.

Cliff Schimmels
Wheaton, Illinois
1991

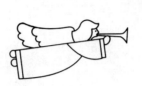

Sunday School memories —
poignant pictures from childhood,
nostalgia for an institution
as it was in our experience.
This is what Cliff Schimmels
draws on for this warmhearted book.

Sunday School began in 1780 in England,
under the direction of Robert Raikes, to
give religious training to working children.
Soon, churches were sponsoring the schools,
and in the newly formed country of America,
Sunday Schools became a distinctive element
of most Protestant congregations.

Sunday School — why is it so special?
The gathering of children?
The teachers who loved us?
The songs and stories?
The pictures to take home?
All of these, but most of all the caring.
In Sunday School we learned,
better than we knew at the time,
about life and love, and about
God's long intentions toward us.

The Lesson of
THE UNBELIEVABLE

"WHAT DID YOU LEARN IN SUNDAY SCHOOL?" a father asked his son.

With a shrug of his shoulders and the tone of a child who has often been so questioned, the young boy said, "She told us about Moses crossing the Red Sea."

"Oh," the father inquired with eagerness, "what did she say?"

The boy paused only for a second and began the narrative. "Well, it seems like this fellow Israel had a whole bunch of children who were being held hostage by this guy Pharaoh. Well, old Moses got mad about that and went to this guy Pharaoh and gave this ultimatum. He warned him that if he didn't let those people go, he would be in big trouble. So Pharaoh said, 'Okay, you can leave.' Then Moses loaded all Israel's children in big buses and started off.

"Well, old Pharaoh thought about what he had done and changed his mind. He called out his army and tanks and half-tracks and big guns and began chasing old Moses.

"When Moses and all those children got to the Red Sea, they knew they were trapped and had to do something. So they decided to sandbag that old Sea. They sandbagged two sides all the way across. Then they got centrifugal pumps and pumped all the water out so that they could go through on the seabed.

"But they weren't finished. They put big explosives all through those sandbags, and when Pharaoh's army and machines started down through the Sea, the Children of Israel detonated those explosives with this remote device over on the other shore, blew up the sandbags, and destroyed Pharaoh's army."

"Wait a minute," the father protested with deep concern. "Is that the way she told the story?"

"Naw," said the boy with another shrug. "But if

14

I told you the story the way she did, you'd never believe it."

And that's the first lesson of Sunday School. You have to learn to believe the unbelievable.

The curriculum is filled with such stories. The sea parted, the walls fell down, the clothes didn't wear out, the sun stood still, the lame man walked, the fishnets didn't break, and the virgin gave birth.

The whole church is filled with the stories of the unbelievable. Mrs. Metcalf had polio when she was a little girl. The doctors said she would never walk again, but now she doesn't even limp. Mr. Robinson was once a brawler and a drunk, but now he isn't.

Sunday School is about both kinds of stories because it's about the power of God at work in ordinary people.

For me, Sunday School is more than a refreshing experience. In the Sunday School stories, past and present, is the sap of my spiritual fervor.

In recent years, I have come to believe that the natural passages of life turn us all into autobiographers. It is during these landmark or crises times that we remember our own histories—

who we are and how we got to be this way.

Not long ago, I crossed a pleasant passage and gained a new name. I became someone's "Grandpa," and from this joy, I have found it delightfully necessary to make a mental list of all those times and people who have contributed to my being and becoming. I owe them all my gratitude. But in the midst of remembering moments complex and simple, of remembering lessons painful and pleasant, I have most frequently caught myself recalling Sunday School. From earliest boyhood to last week, the memories flow and tumble, fleeting from year to year, and even decade to decade.

Some of those great lessons I caught at first impact, but others I didn't comprehend until that special moment years later when, during my quiet contemplation, God gave me insight and brought meaning to a memory.

It's through such moments that I have come to see special significance and truth in a popular title rephrased to meet my personal pilgrimage. Everything I really need to know, I learned in Sunday School.

But the big lesson was that I learned to believe the unbelievable.

The Lesson of
THE BACK ROOM

THE OTHER DAY a woman called to invite me to come to her church to speak to the Little Children's Sunday School Class.

I accepted immediately. Speaking to the Little Children's Sunday School Class is top priority with me. I seize any opportunity that has possibility of "touching the future," as one teacher put it. Besides that, my mind works at the level of little children.

Because I had never been to her church before, the caller volunteered to meet me at the front door so that she could help me find the classroom.

"I don't think that will be necessary," I answered as politely as I could, but with a ring of confidence that surprised even me. "I'm sure I can find it on my own. I'll just go to the very back room."

There was silence on her end for a moment; then she chuckled. "You're right, but how did you know?" she asked, in the kind of tone that assured me that she really didn't expect an answer.

She was fortunate to communicate that tone. I do have an answer to her question, but it would take me at least an hour to deliver it. After all, it took me a lifetime to gather it, and I still get a bit emotional with any provocation to recount why I know where the Little Children's Sunday School Class is.

Any time we ponder such matters as this and think of how we know what we know, and how we got to be who we are, the word *first* becomes one of the major terms of our vocabulary. It keeps popping up everywhere.

One of the common activities of personality assessment is to recall our very first memory. We hold special our first bout with romance. God sent word to the church at Ephesus that He was upset with them because they had forsaken their first love.

In matters spiritual and religious, our very first experiences are not only the openings into the new and abundant life, but they also become doormen supervising and directing the entrance of all subsequent experiences. The special places with their own special sights and sounds and odors live active lives in our storehouse of memories long after other memories have faded into oblivion.

With those first impressions right at the threshold of our consciousness, we remember how Sunday School should look, and we remember how Sunday School should smell. And now years and decades and scores later, our senses will catch a faint whiff of the stuff of first experiences, and all the memories will come tumbling back as fresh as on the day of origin. We catch a quick glance or smell, and we say, "Now that's Sunday School."

In the same way, the special people with their quirks and habits and talents and smiles and tears become the people appropriate to Sunday School experiences at all times and places, and we find ourselves hoping that our children and grandchildren can have a teacher just like our very first and can know classmates like those in our first class.

Those first places and people become proto-
types. Years later, we may become bold enough to
experiment with alternate structures and places,
but we experiment with the security of the memory of the first.

I first found the happiness of learning about the
Lord in a small country church which sat serenely
in the middle of a fertile valley. The hills which
served as sentries both on the east and west were
aesthetically decorated with red dirt, green grass,
and frequent outcroppings of white gypsum. The
valley, long and slender, was like a beehive of
plant life buzzing with cotton, corn, wheat, and
alfalfa.

The church building itself was unmistakably *the*
church building of the community. It was stately
and tall, painted white and well-kept. Built on the
only little rise in the valley, it could be seen from
almost every farm home, as if it were a standing
symbol of centrality. Even strangers driving
through the community could glance in that direction and know immediately that this was the
church.

As I remember it through boy eyes, it was a

gigantic building, with rooms spacious and plentiful; in truth, it was one big room with a network of curtains which could be pulled in a variety of ways to create separate spaces which could be imagined into rooms with the individual traits and flaws which make rooms significant in our memories.

For learning, our Sunday School was divided into two general sections — adults and children. At the very beginning of each Sunday morning, the curtains were pulled to divide the church into two rooms where each group had a general opening exercise where we sang together, had a short introduction to the lesson, took up the offering, each put money in the birthday bank one Sunday a year, and prayed.

Then the back part where the children met was further divided into three more classrooms as sturdy as curtains and imaginations could make them, one for the school-age boys, one for school-age girls, and one for the little children — those who had not yet learned to read. Of course, the little children went into the very back room. I'm sure there was a reason for that in the beginning; but even after the original reason had been lost somewhere in the passing of the years, and the new reason had become "just because," the little children still met in the back room.

The people of our church and of my first experiences came from all over the valley, and they came in great hordes. Not long ago I saw the actual statistics and realized that the record attendance for that great horde was sixty-seven on a Sunday when we had a special preacher coming. But sixty-seven is a relative number, and to a boy in the midst of his first experience, that was a great horde.

Most of those people had been born in the valley and had lived there all their lives, and they brought to our church the riches of diversity. There are those who would tell us that there can't possibly be any diversity in a crowd of people who live in the same spot and do the same things for a living and have similar last names.

But I learned early that diversity is the product of perspective and not circumstance. Each person there had a unique relationship with God and a unique relationship with the world, and that uniqueness provided enough diversity to hold me in a state of awe as I sat in classes or listened to the conversations, or discovered the majesty and reality of God during the open testimony times. Regardless of what experiences and teachers I might know in the years to follow, I shall never forget some of those early lessons that those people taught me from their diversity.

Mrs. Smith was in charge of the children's section, conducted the opening exercise, and taught the school-age girls. She was a pleasant woman who could be firm. Perhaps that is why she was so good at what she did. She had a look that could control us and a heart big enough to hold us.

Mrs. Smith was an expert in the Epistles. Regardless of the nature of the lesson for the day, she could find something from one of Paul's letters that would not only relate but contribute to our understanding. From her I learned to love his letters.

Mrs. Murphy, who taught the school-age boys, was an expert in the Old Testament, particularly the history part. She not only knew the names of all the kings, but she even knew in what order they came and whether they were good or bad.

From her as much as from any teacher I have ever had anywhere or anytime, I learned the lesson of the reality of the past. Each Sunday I came to realize that the people of the Bible were more than fictional characters in fairy tales. They were real. They ate and had children and had disputes with their children, and they cried and died.

After all these years, I will sometimes flip through those pages of my Bible which are still a bit slick with newness in far-off spots such as 1 Chronicles, and I will remember Mrs. Murphy, and I will resent my schedule which will not permit me the hours needed to relive and learn.

Mrs. Henderson, the other person in our children's section, owned the back corner. She taught the little children and was synonymous with that back corner. Since she had walls plus a curtain, she decorated with permanent posters and charts, and had class longer than anybody else.

Mrs. Henderson was the church grandmother. Some of the children were actually her very own grandchildren, but the rest of us didn't know which ones they were. She was everyone's grandmother who brought cookies and spiritual concern.

Mrs. Henderson loved the prophecy part of the Bible, and was a scholar in that area. Even during the war years when some items of luxury were scarce, Mrs. Henderson had a battery and her radio worked. So she listened and brought the rest of us reports, not only of the news of the world, but of the wisdom of the radio preachers who in those days were quite concerned about biblical prophecy.

Sometimes as we get older, it's hard to discern what impact some event or some person years before has had. To this day, I am not sure I know the significance of why I remember Mrs. Smith's purple dress, or Mrs. Murphy's sense of humor, or the mole on Mrs. Henderson's chin. Recollections of other people that have come between then and now have faded into faintness. Maybe I remember because they were the first, and they remind me of something bigger and more precious.

My prayer is that Jesus won't ever find a need to send to me the reprimand that he had to deliver to those people at Ephesus. To make sure that I don't lose the memory of the joy of the energy of that first love, I will give it the structure of the

27

lessons of people and places who filled that time for me. And that's how I know where the little children meet.

 *The Lesson of*
SINGING BEFORE
STUDYING

SUNDAY SCHOOL CEREMONIES come in two types. There are those which are temporary. They come and go, drifting in from season to season or year to year or director to director.

But there are those ceremonies which are permanent. They span seasons and years and generations and endure attacks and diseases and pressures.

These permanent ceremonies come in two types. There are those which are authenticated and documented by Scripture, doctrinal position, or even history. There are others, however, which are permanent on the very convincing logic that this is the way it is supposed to be.

The order of service falls into that last category.

Well, perhaps there is some flexibility in places in the agenda, but there is one permanent principle which has survived all generations and all tests and all trends: You must sing before you study.

There may actually be some biblical support for this. The people in Old Testament days sang at some unusual times. Moses and his people sang out of happiness after they had safely escaped across the Red Sea. David responded to almost all of the human conditions by breaking out into song. He sang when he lost; he sang when he won; he sang when God was happy with him and when He wasn't.

In Sunday School, we sang the first thing. Whether there is significant biblical support for this or not, it served a very real purpose. It woke us up.

Of all the words which we could use to describe that opening song service, the most accurate one would be *hearty*. We sang as if maybe we thought God Himself was a little sleepy on Sunday morning and needed a jolt of shrill sounds.

In Sunday School singing, the whole body must participate. Some of the songs had hand gestures that were as much a part of the song as the words and the tune. No adult who grew up in Sunday School can sing "Deep and Wide" with his hands in his pockets. Another song with hearty hand gestures was, "I'm In Right, Out Right, Up Right, Down Right, Happy All the Time." That one was not only loud and vigorous, but it also required a good deal of room.

Perhaps that's why we Americans seem to need so much personal body space. We grew up singing action songs in Sunday School. When the songs didn't have gestures, we would often invent them, just to show that we were participating.

For the opening ceremonies at our Sunday School, we had piano accompaniment with our singing, but on a limited basis. The only person who could play was Mary Wade, and she could play only in one flat. So Mrs. Smith had to stay up late every Saturday night to make the right selections, and we never got any free sing time.

In those days, when the overhead projector was just so much science fiction, teaching the words of a new song was something of a trial of special gifts. But since Mrs. Smith was both clever and determined, she would write the words with crayons on backs of the rolls of wallpaper that she had left over from decorating. That way, we didn't get the words on some flat surface, but they sort of unrolled in front of us as if we were player pianos responding to cardboard programs.

For me, the song service period was a time for sore ribs. That was not because I sang heartily but because I sang off-key and someone was always poking me. My ability to sing off-key earned me quite a reputation. The kid beside me would stop occasionally and blurt out, "Clifford's singing off-key," and everybody would stare and giggle and still keep going, "I'm in right, out right, up right, down right, happy all the time." But this didn't bother Mrs. Smith. She would nod at me as if it were all right for me to sing off-key as long as I was hearty about it. Of course, at Christmas programs and Rally Days she did ask me just to move my mouth and not let any sound come out. My singing earned me my boyhood nickname, Off-Key Cliff, and I still wear it as a badge of honor.

In spite of my personal successes in the song service, I heartily endorse the principle. Singing before studying is not only a logical order, but it seems to be a natural one as well. Singing stimulates the body, mind, and soul, both for the participant and for the listener. Music, even music that is more hearty than aesthetic, soothes, calms, awakens and refreshes. After having sung together, we could join in and study with a greater sense of genuineness and with the feeling that we were a part of the community; we were not quite as isolated as we had been just a few minutes earlier.

Through my personal research of having thought about this little principle for almost fifty years, I have concluded that singing before studying is still one of the best things we do in Sunday School. I am, in fact, such a strong supporter that I am trying to discover ways to launch this order into other areas of human assembly.

Just for starters, let's think about a court of law. Everybody stands when the judge enters the room and goes to his elevated postion. How would it be if just before he sat down, he would lift his arms in those flowing sleeves and lead everybody in a rousing chorus. I think I would recommend that they all sing,

"My hope is built on nothing less
than Jesus' love and righteousness. . . .
On Christ, the solid rock I stand,
all other ground is sinking sand."

Such a reminder would assure everybody of what justice is. Just maybe after the people had all sung together, they wouldn't get so angry with each other during the court proceedings.

Another place where this principle might have merit would be a space launch. Those are tense times anyway, and a little pre-blast-off singing might do a lot to release anxiety and bring unity. In that case, two songs would seem appropriate, "How Great Thou Art," and "Amazing Grace."

As a person educated in Sunday School ceremonies, I would like to see more singing at summit conferences. Have you ever noticed how weary the participants look, as if they would really rather be back in their rooms taking a nap? If they could just pause in the middle of all their serious deliberations to jump into a chorus or two of "Do Lord" and finish it off with a vigorous rendition of "Deep and Wide," they would feel so refreshed.

I know that I still do at Sunday School, sore ribs and all.

The Lesson of
THE VACANT
FRONT ROW

IN THE THEATER, Front Row Center is the best seat in the house. In the classroom, the eager scholars, the overachievers and those who think their cuteness will appeal to the teacher fight for the front row. At the major leaguer's autograph party, people scramble and trample to get to the front.

In church the front row is unoccupied. I always wondered why that is. At first, I thought that there were doctrinal reasons, but when I got old enough to visit other churches, I learned that this was not just a fact of our local congregation or denomination but was far more global.

Although we didn't know its source or origin, the students in our Sunday School class knew fully the Law of the Vacant Front Row, and we attempted to abide by it in both letter and spirit. But that presented a problem. Ours was a poor church, and we didn't have all that many chairs. Sometimes when we had preaching all day and then dinner on the grounds with large crowds, people would even bring chairs from home just to have a place to sit.

In our class, that shortage was acute. There were just enough chairs for each of us to have one, so during the final prayer of opening exercise, the aggressive would begin to lean and shuffle toward the curtain which designated our Sunday School room, so that on the Amen they could make a break for the second and third rows. The rest of us would straggle in, fight those already there, lose, and wind up sitting on the floor during class. But the front row was still silently and reverently vacant.

Mrs. Murphy wasn't pleased with that arrangement. I think she must have found that teaching boys the purpose of memorizing the books of the Bible in order, while they were wrestling on the floor, was in itself a study in incongruity.

But Mrs. Murphy had a natural teaching gift. This means that she was smarter than boys, even at their own game. She devised a solution. Mrs. Murphy rearranged the room. She placed one lone chair up front right in the middle. Behind it she placed a full row of seats; then she told us that the one lone chair was the front row and the full row was technically the second row. That made sense to us, so we filled all the seats except the one that constituted the front row. After that we all had a seat, except for the Henderson boy who was always late anyway.

Although we accepted her new style of interior decorating, being typical boys we were a bit uncomfortable with the appearance of the strangeness, so we responded with typical boy rebellion. We asked questions — tons and tons of questions. Well, actually we didn't ask a wide variety of questions, but we asked the same question over and over again, and each time we asked it, we had the tone in our voices as if we were the first persons ever to think it, much less to ask.

"Why is the room this way?" "Whose chair is that?" "Who's supposed to sit up there?" "Why is that one seat in the front?"

After Mrs. Murphy had either waited until the level of learning anxiety was appropriate, or had gone totally beserk with all the questions — I couldn't tell which, she decided to turn that one lone chair into a lesson — a powerful and memorable lesson which surely not a single one of us ever forgot.

One morning at about the hundredth repetition of the same question or a reasonable paraphrase, Mrs. Murphy paused, put down her lesson leaflet, and opened her Bible. "Listen carefully," she told us, "and I will explain once and only once about this empty chair." With that announcement, she drew immediate attention, not silent attention, but attention amidst the rustle, because we were excited to get to know this.

Then she began to read to us. From the Book of 2 Kings, one of her favorite books, she read this neat story about a great guy. It concluded, "As they were walking along and talking together, suddenly a chariot of fire and horses of fire appeared and separated the two of them and Elijah went up to heaven in a whirlwind."

That one simple reading provoked a barrage of questions which she answered with an eagerness that showed us that she really enjoyed telling this story to a group of boys who would appreciate it. But as the questions quieted down and as we sat imagining this great scene in our minds, she explained that to this day, Jewish people still expect Elijah to return. Sometimes when they have special feasts and special programs, they reserve a chair at the table to show that they are expecting him to return.

"This chair up here," Mrs. Murphy explained to us, once and for always, "is reserved for Elijah." And she picked up her lesson leaflet and started the class again.

I appreciated the explanation because it clarifies one of the great mysteries in life and worship. That's why churches keep the front row vacant. They want Elijah to have his choice, and from the best seats in the house too.

The Lesson of "YES, MA'AM"

AT OUR HOUSE, we always got our Sunday papers on Saturday night. Out where we lived there was no delivery, so we picked up the paper when we were in town.

There was one advantage to that—we had read the comics by the time we got to Sunday School the next morning. That little opportunity provided one of the highlights of the week. With utter delight, I could sit around and tell the rest of the kids what they could expect. I took special joy in telling the story right up to the punch line and then quitting just in time to make everyone beg for the finish.

In those days one of the our favorite topics in the comics was science fiction, and frequently, the

Sunday morning conversation got around to such wild futuristic speculations as wrist radios and remote control devices. Of course, these were only things of the imagination, too far from reality to be taken with any seriousness, but it was still fun to chat about and to speculate on what life would be like in that way-off future time called the twenty-first century.

One day, right in the middle of our dreaming, Leroy Brady, who buttoned the top button of his sport shirt and did arithmetic problems in his head, startled us all. "I plan to live in the twenty-first century," he boldly proclaimed, and the rest of us hissed and booed.

"Figure it out for yourself," he urged us. So we got the stub pencils they brought to our classroom after they were whittled too short to be used behind the pews anymore, and we figured it out in the margins of the weekly lesson leaflets.

That's when we discovered that most of us would be sixty-three years old when this world entered the twenty-first century. At that time, sixty-three seemed old, but we knew some people who had reached that advanced stage in life, and we decided it really wasn't beyond expectation.

The next problem in our conversation was how we might achieve longevity and actually live to see the future for ourselves. And that's when Mrs. Murphy came to teach. Mrs. Murphy was a good teacher. She studied her lesson well. But she was also a good teacher because she studied the boys well. This day, she sensed something deep was in the air, and she wisely chose to take care of that before she proceeded with the map of Paul's Second Missionary Journey.

"So you want to live to be old?" she asked us, and winced just a bit when we mentioned sixty-three. "Well, let me tell you the way to live a long time."

And we gathered around close as if we didn't want this secret information to slip out to extraterrestrial spies who might be lurking. Besides, Mrs. Murphy was about sixty-three herself. Maybe she really did have a secret. With ears open and eyes bulging like so many bullfrogs, we waited for the formula.

Sensing the seriousness of moment, she bent over and whispered, but loud enough for us all to hear, "Say 'Yes, Ma'am.' " And we waited in the quiet for the rest of it, but there wasn't anymore. She stood up straight, grinned at us and started speaking normally again.

Were we disappointed! We were primed for a secret right out of the science fiction of the comics, and she gave us this. We expressed our disappointment. Loudly and with enthusiasm that grows exponentially in gatherings of boys, we told her of our disappointment.

She laid her finger to her lips to gain silence and asked, "What do you say when your mother tells you to go outside and gather the eggs?"

"Yes, Mother, we will," we all answered in unison with a molasses response, because we knew that this was the kind of answer they expect you to give in Sunday School.

But Mrs. Murphy didn't buy it. "No, what do you really say?" And she left us alone with our own thoughts as we remembered outbursts of disrespect and even rudeness. Then she added, "You really need to learn to say, 'Yes, Ma'am,' and maybe you'll see the twenty-first century."

She opened her Bible and read to an attentive

class of young boys, "Honor your father and your mother, so that you may live long in the land the Lord your God is giving you." Then she added her own comment. "It starts with learning to say a simple 'Yes, Ma'am.' "

Through the years, I have bought the best tapes, read the best books, attended the best seminars and sat under the best teachers in an attempt to learn how to live in a way that would please God. But Mrs. Murphy's prescription still makes about as much sense as anything I have heard since then. "It starts with learning to say a simple " 'Yes, Ma'am.' "

The Lesson of
THE SHOES

WHILE WE WERE GROWING UP, we always had two pairs of shoes. They were named Everyday Shoes and Sunday School Shoes.

We wore Everyday Shoes everyday, and they always took a licking. In those shoes, we kicked clods, climbed trees, chased cows, and did the chores.

We also wore Everyday Shoes to school, so they became a representation of the kind of day we were having. Scuff marks on the right toe reminded us of the joy of getting to the bus stop a few minutes early and having time to engage in a round or two of Kick the Can with brothers or sisters.

Scuff marks on the left toe announced progress

in skill development because we could use both feet to kick the can.

Those were the messages we received from our eyes. Our nose had another story to tell. On some mornings, chores did not go perfectly. On most mornings, chores did not go perfectly. Of all the things pigs are, cooperative is not on the list, and so feeding the pigs was always an adventure frequently documented in after-the-event odors.

But nervous cows could be the most troublesome. They would kick and stomp and swish, and half the milk would wind up on Everyday Shoes instead of in the pail.

In the brisk chill of early morning, that wasn't much of a catastrophe; but about ten o'clock while we were sitting close to a warm radiator trying to learn mental discipline by mastering the sequential steps of long division, that milk stain had a way of awakening the nose and stimulating memories of all mishaps already met that day.

Sunday was different. As usual, we would begin our day with our old friends, Everyday Shoes, but somewhere in the course of the morning would come that poignant moment when it was time to put on Sunday School Shoes.

That moment was like having a miniature Christmas each week. What anticipation! What excitement—to be able to slip our feet into elegance.

But Mother never trusted anticipation alone. That moment was always set in motion by parental reminder which all too often took on the needless tone of reprimand.

"Change your shoes," she would say, in a mood much like that in Indianapolis when the man says, "Start your engines." But before we could race into action, she would offer further explanation. "You don't want to wear those old filthy Everyday Shoes to Sunday School. Jesus is watching."

That's how the transformation occurred every Sunday. Putting on those shoes had special significance. They not only changed our appearance, but they changed our character. They brought an odd combination of reverence and joy to our lives.

The demands of temptation were still there— the need to giggle when somebody burped during prayer, the need to push when the line to the crayon box got out of control, the need to daydream when the lesson was too long.

But dealing with all that temptation was a bit easier while wearing special shoes that reminded us, "Jesus is watching." Being good brought a special pleasure.

However, the day inevitably came when those two pairs of shoes produced confusion and anxiety. Right in the middle of doing something really important such as kicking a clod or chasing a cow, the sole would break lose on one of the Everyday Shoes and would flap about like the tongue of a collie drinking from the creek. We would then surgically remove the offending part and stuff cardboard inside until we could get to town and buy new shoes.

We never bought new Everyday Shoes. The new shoes were named Sunday School Shoes, and what used to be Sunday School Shoes were reassigned and rechristened Everyday Shoes.

That's when the theological confusion began. Wearing those shoes had always brought a sense of reverence to our existence. We knew that Jesus was watching. Mother told us that. And we could curb most of our normal impulses for the duration. But now what did we do?

For three days after that transition, we walked around in our Puritan faces and modified behavior, living constantly under the ever watchful eye of Jesus.

Now that middle age and middle class have invaded my life, I have three pairs of shoes and I haven't designated any one as Sunday School Shoes. But I have learned to live with the dilemma.

Mother's reminder was accurate; it just needed extending. Jesus is watching while we are wearing Sunday School Shoes. But He also is watching when we are wearing Everyday Shoes, or even going barefoot, for that matter.

Jesus told us this Himself when He said, "And surely I am with you always, to the very end of the age."

That isn't a threat. It's a promise.

The Lesson of
THE OLD MARE

ONE OF THE MOST IMPORTANT LESSONS I
ever learned in Sunday School, and one that I find
myself using frequently, was a lesson my father
taught me — and he wasn't even there.

One day I rode The Old Mare to Sunday
School. No, the capital letters are not mistakes.
That was the horse's name. At our house, we
didn't stay awake late at night trying to name our
animals. We had a dog named Dawg. We had a
cow named The Heifer. When that animal got to
be twenty-one years old and one of the oldest
cows in captivity, we still called her The Heifer.

As I said, I rode The Old Mare to Sunday
School. In those days, riding a horse to Sunday
School was the equivalent of taking the limo to-

day. We lived three miles away, and on most Sundays we had to walk. On some Sundays, we rode The Old Mare, but I had to ride with my older brother and sister, and that was more like going on the bus. It was faster than walking, but not much. And it was terribly crowded. I had to hang on tight just to keep from getting killed.

On this day, I rode The Old Mare by myself. We always had a rule at our house that when we rode a horse and tied her up for some time, we took the bridle off. Some folks' horses could drink through the bits, but our horses never could master that little art. We took the bridle off so The Old Mare could keep her tummy full of water, drinking from the tub out by the tree where we all tied our horses during Sunday School and church.

On the day of the big lesson, I dawdled some on my way. Actually, I stopped to chase a coyote, and when I finally got to Sunday School, I could tell that I was almost late. One of the Henderson kids was already scampering across the lawn, so I knew I was in trouble. I didn't want to be late to class. I didn't want to be embarrassed, walking in behind a Henderson, and also I was worried that God would mind. That's when I made a big mistake. I didn't bother to take the bridle off. I just rushed into Sunday School and started singing and praying and studying as if I were holy.

But I couldn't get my mind off The Old Mare, standing out under that tree in the warm April wind without any means of getting at the water. And the thought pestered me all through Sunday School, all through the song service, all through the preacher's message which was particularly long this day and seemed even longer with me trying to concentrate while thinking about that horse. And if that wasn't bad enough, we had Communion that day.

We never had Communion except on the Thursday night before Easter, but that Sunday we had Communion. I wasn't really attentive because I was thinking about poor Old Mare. I tried to get my mind off her by remembering Bible verses, but the only thing I could think of was verses which pertained to this. Wrestling with my guilt, I might have paraphrased a bit as I recalled such past lessons as, "When the ox is in the ditch, common sense is more important than laws." Or, "Do unto your horse as you would have your horse do unto you."

And I thought of the day I would stand before Jesus and He would say, "I was thirsty and you didn't even take the bridle off."

Frightened and guilt-ridden, as soon as I heard "Amen," I leaped out of my seat and ran out to that tree prepared to take the bridle off and, like Zaccheus, make restitution for my past sins. But, alas, the other horses had already drunk all the water in the tub, and I had to ride The Old Mare all the way home in the heat and wind.

When I got home, I rode her right straight to the tank; I pulled the bridle off, and she started to drink. And she drank and drank and drank. She drank with such force that her sides would heave, and she'd snort water out her nose. Then she would pause, lift her head up, and stare at me with those sad eyes of hers and drink some more.

My father came out of the house, walked out to where we were, stood and watched and didn't say a word. I bowed my head and waited for the on-slaught, the almost welcome reprimand that I was going to get for my sins. But he didn't say a word.

He just watched. When The Old Mare had finally managed to restore her system, we started to the barn, and my father came along side of me. "Did you learn anything in Sunday School today?" he asked in a tone made threatening by its calmness.

"Yes, Sir," I said with my head down so I couldn't look at him. And that was the last time he ever mentioned it.

A few years ago, God called me to deliver the Sunday sermon at a nearby church. About eight o'clock on Saturday night, I sat down with my commentaries and seven translations of the Scripture to put the finishing touches on what had the potential of being an oratorical and theological masterpiece.

Just then the phone rang. Our friends' son was ill at youth camp about three hours away, and they were very worried. Realizing that they were too upset to go alone, my wife and I loaded them into our car and drove the three hours up, spent two hours nursing him, and drove the three hours home.

We got home just in time for me to shower, change my shirt, and go off to church to deliver the great "Unfinished Sermon."

I probably should put a fitting ending on this by telling you that the sermon went off beautifully, but that's not true. It lacked depth and coherence and illustration and energy. And the congregation knew it.

At the end, I stood at the door and shook hands with gracious people who awkwardly fished for something nice to say about the homiletic flop. But while I stood there, I remembered that day years ago when I didn't take the bridle off. I remembered the lesson I had learned, and I realized why I had made my decision the night before.

They also serve God who water horses and take distraught parents on an overnight trip.

The Lesson of
THE RIGHT ORDER

GENESIS, EXODUS, Leviticus, Numbers, Deuteronomy... Mrs. Murphy made us learn the books of the Bible in order. I guess we should have seen it coming. In those days, that assignment was as much a part of Sunday School as singing before you study. Every student in every class in every church in the world, I suppose, learned to say the books of the Bible in order. But like so many things in life, even though it was inevitable, it was still unexpected.

I think she planned it that way. She wanted us to spend our energy learning the books in order, instead of dreading to have to learn them in order. One day she came to class and said simply, "In two weeks, you will have to recite the books of the

Bible in order."

Her announcement came so quickly and easily that we sat stunned. We didn't even have time to bombard her with the customary questions such as, "How are we going to be tested? Do you take off for pronunciation? How many chances do we get?"

In the midst of the surprise and confusion which stifled our creativity, we came up with only one of the usually required questions, "Why are we doing this?" She grinned and said, "It'll be good for you. It'll make your brains grow."

When I got home that noon, my father, fulfilling one of the first requirements of fatherhood, asked, "What did you learn in Sunday School today?"

I answered, "We have to learn the books of the Bible in order." Now that I have become a father, I realize how that answer doesn't quite fit the question which was asked. I'm sure my father was hoping for a discourse on some significant Bible event or character, complete with a description and critical commentary. Now that I'm a Sunday School teacher, I'm sure that she taught us that too. But that isn't what we learned. We learned the assignment, so my answer was actually the correct one.

"Well, good," my father said. "That'll make your brain grow," and he went back to reading the paper.

The next day in school, we held the Sunday School debriefing the very first thing, and because this was a time when I was in my "front row" period, I was the first one questioned. Mrs. Foster looked straight at me and asked, "What did you learn in Sunday School yesterday?"

And I said, "We have to learn the books of the Bible in order."

And Mrs. Foster said, "Well, good. That'll make your brain grow," and with that she went on to the kid behind me.

With no apparent sympathy in sight, I decided that I had no choice but to get on with the task. After all, how tough could this be? There were only sixty-six names to learn, that much I knew, and it seemed that if every adult in the world had learned the books of the Bible in order, surely I could.

But I found this learning activity to be one of

the most difficult assignments I have ever had. It put me into sections of the Bible where I felt like Balboa exploring territory where no human being had ever been before. Perhaps it was the big words and the unusual ways I had to twist my tongue to try to copy what my ear heard when my big brother said them for me. Perhaps it was just the nature of the order itself, but I found the task extremely difficult.

Some books were easier than others. The first five came quickly, but the section with Micah, Nahum, Habakkuk, and Zephaniah required complete concentration, hours and hours of repetition, and the frustration of trial and error. It wasn't just these obscure spots that caused trouble. I had a time with Ephesians, Colossians, Philippians, and Galatians too. I also got fooled in those places where I thought it would be easy. I liked those spots where there is a First and a Second, and breezed through those feeling almost as if I were cheating or least getting a bonus point. But then I ran into the First, Second, and Third, and had to work at remembering which was which.

When the day of oral exams came, I was prepared but not confident. Since the testing was to be in public and we had the luxury of learning from everyone who had gone before, I prayed that God would allow me not to be first. He heard and answered. We drew numbers out of the box, and I was fourth. That was the right number. I would have the value of listening to those earlier ones and still be far enough up into the list that I wouldn't be worn out when it came my time.

As the three students in front of me recited, I listened, but only with one ear because I was still cramming. When it came my turn, I made it all the way up to the trouble spot of those last books of the Old Testament, and with concentration and by reading Mrs. Murphy's facial response, I made it all the way through without a single mistake. I was so pleased with myself. In fact, I was proud. I started into the New Testament and said, "Matthew, Luke, John," and those who had already finished and were listening more than the others caught my mistake and laughed. I was embarrassed and flustered. Mrs. Murphy only smiled and said, "That's all right. Go on." But that was the problem. I couldn't go on. When they laughed,

I lost my rhythm and couldn't remember where I was at all. Again, she saw my plight and said, "That's all right. Just start over again."

So I did. "Genesis, Exodus, Leviticus, Numbers . . ."

It's funny how little things become your reputation. You could live your whole life being brilliant and diligent and talented, and one slip of the tongue becomes your legacy. One moment of misunderstanding and people will remember you forever. I thought that was a minor thing at the time, but it hasn't turned out that way. That's part of the lore of the valley now. People tell their grandchildren about me, or at least about the day I had to start over again. At reunions, this is the remembered topic. And I thought I was doing what she had asked.

Despite that, I still believe in the assignment. If I could make a prescription for all fourth graders in this nation, I would have them learn the books of the Bible in order. I do think the reason is greater than pure spite. . . . "If I had to, so should they."

I have found that mastery to be one of the most

profitable pieces of mental machinery I possess. I am fairly good in Sword Drill games, and I can find the text when the preacher announces it. But it's deeper than that. Knowing the books in order is an entryway into the Scriptures themselves. We could be good Bible scholars without knowing the right order, but just having this knowledge is a reminder that we *should* know and that we *can* know.

The other day, I read the local newspaper with an intensity somewhere between casual and slightly interested, and I counted twenty-seven references to the Bible. I found myself feeling sorry for people who don't know the books of the Bible in order or who don't have some other tool for studying the greatest Book of all. They obviously would have missed those allusions, references, and analogies, and their reading of the newspaper would have been less than what it might have been.

It occurred to me that day that we actually cheat our children when we don't require them to learn the books of the Bible in order. Besides that, it would make their brains grow.

The Lesson of
THE BROKEN
CRAYONS

COLORING was not my favorite thing to do. It didn't even make the top ten. On a list of irregular duties and responsibilities, coloring was down around getting knots out of shoelaces when I was in a hurry to go swimming and pulling cockleburs out of cows' tails.

Just the thought of coloring in Sunday School was enough to haunt me awake at least twice every Saturday night with a jolt loud enough to wake up my brother and any other assorted animal life that happened to be sleeping in or around our bed.

The reason for my fear was justified — the result of a blending the natural and the theological.

In His infinite wisdom, God saw fit to make me an upside-down left-hander. Actually, I'm not so sure whether it was God's design or my childish invention born out of necessity to write with some hand. Since I didn't know the difference between left and right, the pencil just sort of wound up in my left hand, and I turned my hand upside down for better control.

That's how it happened. To some it might seem so very natural, but I still feel that it was providential, and all those people who have laughed at my penmanship through the years will someday answer for their sins.

My coloring was not only awkward but messy. And Sunday School coloring was the worst. Every Sunday morning there would come that dramatic moment in the lesson when Mrs. Murphy—or sometimes Mrs. Smith—would roll her eyes around the room, grin rather falsely, and exclaim, "Have you ever wondered what those people in your lesson today must have looked like?"

In later years as I have acquired a taste for big words, I have learned that educators call this moment and its subsequent activity "visualization." The teachers themselves call it "time off."

The reaction was always the same. All the other

children would wiggle with glee, and I would sit in utter dread as the teacher distributed sheets of paper with faint outlines of the heroes of the day.

Then, amidst the wiggle, she would give the magic signal, "You may go get crayons now." And the herd would rush full speed ahead to the cigar boxes in which a giant assortment of crayons, present, past, and a long time ago were stored. Have you ever wondered what would have happened in those days to Sunday School, and elementary education in general if there had been no cigar boxes?

Of course, the aggressive ones would get to the boxes first and rummage with the intent of a shopper at a clearance sale until they found not only the choicest colors but also the longest and newest.

By the time the timid and the coloring haters got a turn to look, there remained only the stubby and broken bits of what used to be. Those broken pieces of color stuffed into my already awkward left hand squelched any Rembrandt fantasies I might have had.

Monochromatic assignments were at least manageable. Things like elephants and sheep and camels and Mt. Sinai allowed me to blob and smear without paying too much heed to that one artistic paradigm above all paradigms, "Stay within the lines."

But multicolored assignments with small spaces brought definition to the label "Fine Arts" and terror to my soul.

One day near Christmas, Mrs. Murphy told us about the wise men who came to visit the Baby Jesus. They were kings, actually, dressed in the richest and brightest colors of the day, and we should color them so.

Now, I ask you, have you ever tried to paint royalty with only an ancient piece of purple crayon?

I managed enough hand control to make the king's cloak purple, but I also managed to make his face purple too. When Mrs. Murphy and the aggressive coloring lovers all laughed and mocked, "Why is his face purple?" I explained that this wise man was happy. After all, he was the one who had brought the myrth.

Coloring poorly does have one serendipitous advantage. It causes one to develop a quick wit.

But this all changed when Edith came to our Sunday School. I never really knew where she came from. She just showed up one day, and about a year later, she disappeared.

Edith was not one of the aggressive ones. In fact, she was so unassuming that we would not even have known her name except that she had to wear a New Person name tag three weeks in a row.

On her first Sunday, when Mrs. Smith asked, "Is there anyone here for the first time?" Walter, who helped Mrs. Smith run things and always got the biggest crayon, pointed to Edith and shouted out loud, "I don't know that girl over there. I've never seen her before." So Edith got to wear the New Person name tag.

The second week she was there, we went through the very same ritual, but on the third Sunday after cheeky Walter said his piece, Mrs. Smith suddenly remembered that she had written the name "Edith" before, and after that, Edith didn't have to wear a New Person name tag.

When it came time to color, Edith didn't rush

with the herd to the storage cabinet. She was so shy she was even behind me. Without a hint of frustration, she reached into the box and took one of the leftover bits. But what happened in the next few minutes revolutionized Sunday School art and the world in general. What Edith did was not only a thing of beauty but it has become a joy forever for all upside-down left-handers everywhere, and in so doing it has authenticated messages on Grecian urns.

With only a nub of a crayon in her hand, Edith proceeded to tear its paper away. She then placed the side of the crayon on the Walls of Jericho and began to move the flat edge around the design.

The result was breathtakingly beautiful. By pressing more firmly on the outside, she created a shading effect; and with the continuous motion, she eliminated the telltale blotches of children's art. And all the while, she stayed within the lines.

Besides that, she was the first one finished. When Mrs. Smith held up Edith's work for all to see and admire, the room was filled with another color, the green of aggressive kids shown up at their own game.

And the world laughed joyously.

After that, even the aggressive kids picked the broken crayons, but they could never reach Edith's level because she was the master.

Through the years, this lesson of Edith and the broken crayon has been good for me. Although I don't always achieve the full power of the insight, the image is still with me, still haunting me with memories of delight and the joy of flexibility.

How often life deals us a broken crayon!

The dentist says, "I'm sorry. This is not your normal, run-of-the-mill cavity. This one requires ROOT CANAL."

You're in a hurry to a very important meeting with a very important person when you spot that cheery sign, "Road Construction Ahead."

The salesman says, "If you can't afford this one, I have another model almost as nice."

The boss asks, "Could you have it by Monday?"

That teenager who is your very own flesh and blood, your posterity and hope, has a total vocabulary of three phrases, "Everybody else will be there," "That's not fair," and "You don't trust me."

At such moments I remember the Sunday School lesson from the day when Edith taught me to tear the paper off the crayon and make a beautiful picture anyway.

Somebody who was really good at this was a fellow named Paul. He wasn't particularly handsome. As a speaker, he was so naturally gifted and dynamic that one night part of his audience went to sleep and fell out the window. He was always getting beaten up or shipwrecked or run out of town.

But in the midst of all this adversity, he wrote a letter to a group of people in Rome who weren't exactly living in the Ritz themselves. He said, "For we know that all things work together for the good of those who love God and are called according to His purpose."

The Lesson of
KNOWING IN PART

LIKE CIVILIZATIONS and countries and even families, Sunday Schools have histories. Sometimes the history of a Sunday School is written down, like the history of a country. And sometimes, like the history of a country, the history of a Sunday School contains the detailed accounts of wars and civil wars.

But Sunday Schools also have unwritten histories. Usually, the stuff of the unwritten histories is of the mishap variety—the accounts of people doing and saying the strangest things. These gather through generations and become part of the legend of the place. Most of these events are factual, real happenings to real people, but once they are inducted into the legendary hall of honor and go through frequent repeatings, the real facts may be revised, edited, and embellished in the name of good storytelling.

The following story is a part of the legend of the Sunday School of my childhood. Although the story is said to have happened even before I was born, I have heard it repeated so often that I now have a vivid memory of all the details as surely as if I had been there myself.

Charles Ray Lambert didn't come to Sunday School much. For one thing, he lived way out on the edge of the valley; and for another, he really didn't seem all that interested. Charles Ray didn't come enough to learn the etiquette of the place. He even wore his Everyday Shoes. When he did come, the teachers acted really excited to see him, but most of the other children just seemed to ignore him.

One day when Charles Ray was there, Mrs. Murphy, who was theologically committed to the principle of biblical memorization, assigned the class the task of learning her favorite passage, Psalm 23. Everybody was to work on it all week and next Sunday there would be a time for us to recite.

Well, on the next Sunday, Mrs. Murphy could tell that no one was familiar enough with the entire passage to risk it alone, so she had the class recite together. That way, individual students could hide in places of limited knowledge and she could still tell where the trouble spots were when the unison speech dimmed from vigorous clarity to quiet mumbling.

But those moments followed a pattern. The recitation smacked of confidence in the beginning, faded some during that middle part about the table and head, and picked up steam again for the finale.

When it was over, the class stood in satisfaction of what they had accomplished, but Jimmy Joe White, who was standing next to Charles Ray, asked loudly, "What did you say?"

Charles Ray answered in a defensive tone, "I said it." Of course, most of the students doubted this. They doubted that Charles Ray had even studied Psalm 23. In fact, most of them doubted that Charles Ray even had a Bible, although he said he did, a big white Bible with red letters and everything, but too big to carry to Sunday School.

"Say it for us, Charles," they all insisted. "Say that last part for us."

And Charles bowed his head and repeated what he thought he had heard. "And surely, good Mrs. Murphy will follow me all the days of my life."

That moment is part of the unwritten history of our Sunday School. The name of Charles Ray Lambert lives from generation to generation, and people young enough to be his grandchildren still tell the story and laugh heartily.

Everybody loves that story, except maybe Charles Ray. He never came back to Sunday School after that day in the limelight and he left the community when he was sixteen, never to return.

I can understand his plight and I'm not sure he needed to be all that embarrassed. For Charles Ray spoke for many of us, maybe most of us, that morning years ago, when he got enough courage to repeat for the public what he thought he had heard.

How often we hear only in part! How often we know only in part! How often, like Charles Ray, we send the concept from our eyes or ears to our brain in some sort of fog and haze, thinking all the time that we know the truth clearly.

One day, Jesus taught a great lesson about the promise of His Father's mansion and the joy of living there forever. But Thomas didn't get it. He couldn't comprehend and needed more explanation. So Jesus answered in words that made perfect sense to some, "I am the way, the truth, and the light."

But Thomas' later actions after the Crucifixion and Resurrection indicated that he didn't get that either. He was still in a fog when he came one day and demanded to touch the nail holes and inspect the damage.

Through thirty-seven years of learning what it means to live with Jesus within me, I have come to believe that much of Christian growth is this business of examining and rethinking basic ideas. How often I pick up my Bible to have it flop open to some familiar spot. How often I say, "I've already read these words at least a thousand times. I even have them memorized and can say them by heart." But how often I read anyway to discover a truth I have never seen before and then realize that all these years I have been reciting something that sounds like, "And surely good Mrs. Murphy shall follow me all the days of my life."

After we have finished laughing at the legend, perhaps we should bow our heads and ponder the lesson that Charles Ray Lambert taught us that day.

The Lesson of
SHORT PRAYERS

THOSE "OLOGISTS" who stay up late at night to ponder why humans act the way they do should spend some time studying why certain people get called upon most often to pray in church services.

When we were in the Kids Sunday School World, we had two out-loud prayers.

In the "huddled masses" meeting just before we broke away and ran off to our classes, we were led in prayer by either Mrs. Henderson or Mrs. Smith.

Mrs. Henderson was an old woman. Well, maybe she wasn't old all her life, but it seemed like she was.

Mrs. Henderson always taught the "younguns," those kids who couldn't read yet, and she knew a lot about God. When she led in prayer, she told

God what she knew about Him. She knew a lot about the Bible, and when she led in prayer, she told God what the Bible said. She knew a lot about the world, and when she led in prayer, she told God what was going on in the world, as if it would come as a surprise to Him.

And Mrs. Henderson prayed on and on and on and on.

With our heads bowed and our eyes closed, we stood and stood and fought the anxiety to get to class. We always lost. For one thing, our feet began to hurt and our legs got tired. I'll never understand the reason for this. Boys can run and jump and kick clods and play for hours and not lose control of the calf muscles. But standing still for a five-minute prayer brings exquisite torture to the lower extremities.

After we stood on tired legs with our eyes closed for so long, we would begin to get dizzy. The world would spin, and we would lose our balance and begin to reel. And then we would bump into the kid next to us who was reeling some too. And he would push us, and we would push back. And about the time Mrs. Henderson was ready to tell God what was happening in the rest of the world, major conflict was erupting behind the curtain that turned our church into Sunday School rooms.

It wasn't just the idea of two kids wrestling that was so bad, but it was two kids wrestling with their heads bowed and eyes closed.

If these events are ever recorded in history, they will be called "The Wars of No Fair Peeking."

Mrs. Smith, who taught older kids, understood boys; and when she prayed, she prayed short. We didn't have time to get into tired legs or spinning worlds or wrestling matches. We just prayed and went to class.

It was during this period of my life that I grew to appreciate short prayers. As is often the case in theology, the reasons were practical at first, but later I searched the Scriptures until I found support.

When Paul was on his way to Damascus to do a little dirty work, he was stopped along the way by a light and a voice from heaven. From a prayerful posture of lying flat on the ground, he cried out to Jesus, "Who are You, Lord?"

The publican, with his head bowed out of humility and not duty, said, "God, have mercy on me, a sinner."

The leper kneeled in front of Christ and said, "Lord, if You are willing, You can make me clean."

Twenty-one words in all three, yet what else is there to say about the revelation of God, the power of God, and the will of God? It doesn't take so many words when you choose them well.

There are times in my life when I need the Mrs. Henderson style prayers, and I am glad for what she taught me years ago in that Sunday School opening assembly.

There are times when I need to kneel, bow my head, close my eyes to all distractions, and open my ego and essence to God. There are times when I need to lose track of minutes and even hours and give all the energy within me to the task of talking with God.

But there are times that I need the shorter version. I encounter events which require God's attention, but for which I do not have time for sufficient preparation or proper posture.

Just the other day, I was motoring along when two lanes blended into one, and some fellow in a Ford Taurus cut me off causing me to brake in a dangerous way.

At that particular instant, I needed to call on the power of God, but if I had kneeled and bowed my head, I would have probably wiped out half a city block and a few dozen people.

Instead, with eyes wide open, I did a little para-phrase of the leper's request, "Lord, if You are willing, You can cleanse me of my vengeful thoughts," and He did. And then I pronounced another prayer. "Thank You for sending Mrs. Smith to teach me how to pray."

The Lesson of
LOOKING AHEAD

MRS. FOSTER was my first grade teacher, and second grade, and third, and fourth. In our one-room schoolhouse, she taught all eight grades.

Because she was a typical teacher and we were typical students, we always knew what upset her. She didn't like it at all when we tripped or pushed during the recess basketball game, particularly when we were guarding her. She got upset when we didn't wipe our feet before coming back into the building after we had played Dare Base out in the mud. She yelled a lot if we left our half-eaten lunches in the cloakroom overnight and the mice got in. She didn't appreciate snakes in the schoolyard, and it always upset her for us to peek ahead in our books.

Sometimes we would try it when we were at the library. I just used the word "library" to make this sound more cultured and to make my schooling sound more credible. The library at our school was a steel cabinet full of books up at the front of the room.

Since the students in all eight grades used the same cabinet, Mrs. Foster usually supervised the time any one student would spend in the selection process.

But we would sometimes take advantage. If we thought she wasn't looking, we would slip out a book and browse. Usually the most appealing books for browsing were those volumes reserved for the people older than we were, unless, of course, we were in the eighth grade. Then we could browse in the first grade books.

But since this browsing time was guarded and precious, we would sneak our peeks at the last page. If the best part of a joke is the punch line, then surely the best part of a book is the last page. However, if Mrs. Foster caught us doing this, she would come by and thump the backs of our heads like they were ripe watermelons.

Then she would say, "Don't look ahead. You'll spoil the story." That's what she would always say—the same thing over and over again. With that kind of repetition, those seven words became more than just a reprimand, a reminder, or a lesson. They became a creed, a conscience; the rest of our lives we might peek ahead, but we would feel guilty about it with the voice of Mrs. Foster ringing in our ears and the memory of sharp pain banging on the backs of our heads.

But in Sunday School I confronted another lesson. It first happened on the day I gained the wonderful insight that the lesson leaflet they handed us every Sunday morning was actually somehow related to that big black Bible Mrs. Murphy carried to class.

It was one of those significant "Ah ha!" moments of truth that come along periodically in our development and leave us wiser and more mature in their wake.

I am not even sure I know what triggered the insightful moment. I don't really recall any process of preparing the fertile field for learning unusual circumstances or specific teaching techniques.

At the time we were studying the life of King David. It seemed we had studied the life of David for the last six years, but it was probably more like three months.

On this day our leaflet was titled, "1 Kings 2:1-10, The Death of David," and in the last lines we read, "Then David rested with his fathers and was buried in the City of David."

Even at my young age, I knew that this would be the final chapter for old King David. Once you're buried, you don't get much written about you. I just knew that was the end of that story, and I went about the business of wondering who would be the hero of the next story.

Mrs. Murphy, also at a transition, closed her big black Bible and laid it on the empty front row chair just in front of me.

Being a kid afflicted with a normal amount of curiosity, I yielded to the urge to look in that book myself. (Years later, I have learned that yielding to curiosity is called research.)

I flipped open the book to a random spot and read "1 Kings 2 – The Death of David." It was the same as the leaflet! I read on and saw the very same words we had been reading all morning. Finally, I came to the end of the story. ". . . and was buried in the City of David." Suddenly, it all made sense. The reason she had been reading the book was that it was the same as the lesson leaflet. Then I caught a grasp of the truth—the lesson leaflet had been taken from the Bible.

At that point, I got my taste of utter frustration. I had just learned something profound and deep and life-changing—something that deserved to be shouted from the mountaintop. But I was afraid to whisper it for fear that I was the only one in the whole class who hadn't known that fact in the first place.

But that wasn't the biggest shock. With a strong mental image of my schoolteacher causing me great feelings of guilt, I decided to peek ahead. When no one was watching, I would look up the next story and get a jump on the class for the weeks to come.

Rather than seeming too obvious, I grabbed a bundle of pages of the Bible the size that I could get between my thumb and forefinger, flipped over, and read, "Psalm 34—A Psalm of David."

"Wait a minute," I shouted to myself in the forced silence of my own guilt. "We've finished the story on David. Why is there more?" But there was more. That whole book was filled with the poems that were obviously written by David. I was fascinated with the possibility.

I couldn't wait to get to school the next morning. In those days, the first thing we did every Monday morning was to have a Sunday School debriefing. Mrs. Foster would move from seat to seat and ask each student for a full report. We would recite Bible verses, summarize themes, or explain some interesting piece of history or geography. This was a good way to make the transition from weekend to school week; we learned some Bible verses, but most importantly we learned the embarrassment of skipping Sunday School.

This particular Monday morning, I was prepared for the debriefing period. I had imagined how Mrs. Foster would look when I said it. She too would surely be surprised with my discovery.

So I explained what I had done, not leaving out a single detail. I explained how we studied the death of David. With only a hint of fear of correction, I told of peeking ahead. With enthusiasm, I revealed that there was more to the story and that maybe peeking ahead would not be wrong but even profitable.

Having delivered my story, I sat back waiting for Mrs. Foster to be as shocked as I was. But she wasn't. She only smiled and said, "Oh, yes, the Bible is different from any other book. It's even more exciting when you know how it's going to come out."

With that, she moved on to the kid behind me.

The Lesson of
ROLLIE

ROLLIE WAS NOT a typical boy, but his story is typical because in every community and every Sunday School there is at least one person who finds the riches of God in a nontypical way.

From the very first days Rollie began to venture out into public, the whole community realized that he was different. He had an unusual amount of curiosity, more than is normal for a child his age, and unbridled curiosity is often labled something else and blamed for a plethora of strange behavior.

Perhaps his first moment of infamy came from his bout with the clock during his first grade year. Rollie didn't study much. Well, he didn't study the things in the book and on the board. Rollie studied things like Maxine's curls, the bolts in his desk, the cracks in the lump of coal before he put it in the stove, and mouse tracks in the cloakroom.

But these weren't the kinds of studies that thrill teachers, so Rollie got to stay in during recess a great deal of the time. I'm not sure I know what he did during those periods when he was in the building alone or sitting with Mrs. Foster, but I doubt that he studied what was in the book or on the board.

But I do know what he did one particular day. Mrs. Foster was outside playing basketball with the rest of us, and Rollie was in the room alone. That's when he decided to enter the fascinating world of clock repair, or at least clock investigation.

Mrs. Foster's clock was a part of the community legend because she had had it for so long. It was a large black Big Ben that sat up on top of the library cabinet and ticked loudly, particularly during those times when silence seemed to be in order. It sat perched way up out of easy reach because this clock was the official school timepiece, and we ate lunch and went home by the dictates of its ticking.

But that day during recess, Rollie, with his curiosity raging full speed, managed to get the clock down and was well into his third lesson of how the insides worked by the time the rest of us finished basketball and came back in to cipher some before the end of the day. Mrs. Foster was not pleased.

In literary language, this event was a foreshadowing, a sign of things to come. Rollie distinguished himself with such events and matters frequently.

In Sunday School, Rollie was active, and frequently, an active child is renamed The Terror. During opening exercises, he would get down on the floor and crawl around, untying people's shoes and investigating the streaks on the floor. During prayer time, Rollie was always in plain sight when we closed our eyes to start to pray, but he was nowhere to be seen when we opened our eyes, even during Mrs. Smith's prayers which were short.

During class time, Rollie was always the first one to claim a seat, but he never occupied it. He was always up, running around, going into other classes, and crawling on the floor.

99

In the wide open spaces outside the confines of school and Sunday School, Rollie was just as active, but he had more room to spread his behavior around. Rollie once threw a cat off the top of the barn to see if it would land on its feet. He got down on his hands and knees, played like a dog, and chased cars and chickens.

Once when he was a little older, he rigged up an old purse and made it look fat and prosperous and tied a big string on it. One night he put this purse on top of Beaver Creek Bridge, and when people in cars came rumbling by and saw that fat purse, they would screech to a halt and come running back to the promise of riches and prosperity. But just then Rollie would yank the purse off the bridge.

About the time he turned fourteen, Rollie got interested in motorcycles, and that's when the community gave him up as gone for good. He made his first scooter out of an old washer motor and spare parts, but after that he went on to bigger and better things. We lost track of him and didn't even know where he was much of his teen years.

Many years later, I found Rollie again and I know where he is and what he does. He works as a missionary repairman in a remote primitive village in the Amazon jungle, where his curiosity and talent with machinery make him a productive servant in the work of God. He can not only fix anything, but he can also build anything. He still has unlimited energy and works night and day. In other words, God is using him and his ability, all of it.

My story about Rollie isn't all that surprising or ironic. So why bother remembering and telling it? We need to recall it and think about it often, not for the Rollies of our generation, but for those of the next, for those young boys who take clocks apart and crawl on the floor during Sunday School, and for their teachers and parents. This is why people like Mrs. Smith and Mrs. Murphy and Mrs. Henderson get up an hour or two earlier every Sunday for twenty-five years, just to talk a bunch of children into such things as learning the books of the Bible in order and singing "Every day with Jesus is sweeter than the day before."

Even though Rollie spent his time crawling on the floor and disappearing when our eyes were closed in prayer, and even though it didn't seem that he was hearing all that much at the time, I wonder how it would have all come out if Rollie had not been there at all—if there had been no Mrs. Smith who led the singing or Mrs. Murphy who taught about David. Would God now have a servant working on machinery in the Amazon jungle?

Actually, Rollie is not too different from the rest of us. Every one of us is our own Rollie story in a special kind of way. We are the purpose of the energies and the efforts and expenses called Sunday School, but we are more than that. We are also the living examples of the biggest lesson of all, because Sunday School is about the power of Jesus to change people.

We sang a little song about Zaccheus, that wee little man who climbed up into the tree. Jesus changed him. He kept what was good, whacked off what was bad, and turned him into an effective servant.

We read about Peter who denied Christ at His neediest moment. But Jesus changed Him. He kept what was good, whacked off what was bad, and turned him into an effective servant.

Now we study about Rollie and ourselves. Jesus can change us. He can keep what is good, whack off what is bad, and turn us into effective servants.

That's what Sunday School is about.

The Lesson of
THE DINNER TABLES

SOME LESSONS IN LIFE are easy to master. One fact mastered, one trial with correction, and we have a new habit. On the other hand, some lessons are difficult to learn.

Some lessons in life are probably not worth learning. Knowing where the Horse Latitudes are and how they got their name would be advantageous if you happened to get that question in a trivia game; but otherwise, it's just an interesting fact, unless, of course, you're a sailor. On the other hand, some lessons are absolutely valuable to living a worthwhile existence.

The lesson for today is of the second kind on both counts. Not only is it difficult to learn but it is absolutely one of the most important lessons I have ever encountered. After a series of trials and failures, I still wasn't any closer to mastering this seemingly simple concept, until one day in Sunday School class Mrs. Murphy made it all clear for me.

Mine was the last generation of our little church to experience that evangelism strategy called "preaching all day and dinner on the grounds." I think it should be revived.

Several churches would join together and flock to one location. Services would begin about 9 A.M. and go almost until the evening milking time.

Ministers and musicians of every shape and style would expound and deliver and clarify and urge and hold forth, and our souls would be lifted.

But the most memorable part of the day was dinner. With our appetites sharpened by sitting through three sermons, four special music numbers, and hearty congregational singing, we rushed outside on the final "Amen" just to behold the sight.

Tables made out of doors lying across sawhorses seemed to stretch for about three city blocks, and those tables were loaded down with food, but more than just food.

Every human has a "tour de force," and the dishes on those makeshift tables stood as representations of the very finest that every cook in the valley had to offer. This was food at its best, good enough not only to eat, but to autograph. If you picked up any single dish and inspected the bottom, you could find the signature of the author affixed there with cellophane tape.

Although the food had been created by artists, it had been arranged on the table by behavioral scientists, people who understood human appetites and foibles. From the first time I ever attended one of those functions, I knew that salads always came first. Now that I have grown older and understand how scientists work, I even know the reason.

I would tell myself as I started through the food line, "Don't fall victim to this plot. Use discretion. Control your greed." And I started taking a spoonful of this salad and a spoonful of that just to be polite, and maybe a couple of spoonfuls of this particular one because it was my favorite.

But, alas, all too quickly I discovered the finite limits of paper plates. And by the time I had reached the beans and vegetable casseroles, still a good forty feet away from the fried chicken, and sixty feet away from Mrs. Roush's currant pie, I had gone beyond the boundaries of aesthetic food arrangement.

I attended those functions for four years before I even got to taste meat. All the while, I thought it was just my problem. I had no idea that other people, particularly adults who are supposed to be mannerly and disciplined, had the same frustrations.

But one day in class, Mrs. Murphy made herself vulnerable. Good teachers do that occasionally.

We were studying the fourth chapter of Matthew, and old Satan was making it rough on Jesus. First Satan came with food and then with power and finally with wealth. Jesus resisted, and we boys, individually and collectively, were impressed.

"Wow, that's neat," we said, thinking that food, power, and wealth included just about everything that could ever be valuable in life. "He must be strong."

"Yes," she told us, and then she told us something else which I pray that I never forget. "Jesus is more powerful than Satan."

"How powerful is He?" we asked in unison, with images from Captain Marvel comics dancing in our minds.

She paused for a moment, as teachers sometimes do when they confront an unexpected question and have to stall for time and answer. But frightened by the silence, she blurted, almost in embarrassment, what seemed to be the first thing in her mind. "He is so powerful that He could walk right by the salad table."

I knew what she meant!

 # *The Lesson of*
THE LOSER

LET'S START this lesson with a quiz. What's the name of the Bible story about the death of a giant?

I guess that you answered the way I always answered that question, until the Sunday Mrs. Parish came to teach our class.

It was during the flu epidemic, and Mrs. Murphy, the regular teacher, was home sick. Mrs. Smith, the superintendent of the children's division, who substituted at times like these, was out of town tending to her mother who had fallen and broken her hip.

That left the possibility of eight boys caged up in a small room with no supervision. I'm sure that prospect struck terror into the hearts of all those responsible for order in church.

That's when Mrs. Parish was recruited. "Recruited" is an euphemism, an understatement, a gentle way to describe what really happened. In other words, Mrs. Parish was accosted, forced, bribed, and manipulated, and yet, she still managed to smile when she entered the room armed with only a lesson leaflet and the promise that she wouldn't have to do this next week.

The first rule of teaching a class of boys is also the first rule of breaking a colt: "Don't let them see your fear." Mrs. Parish broke the first rule during the opening prayer, and we all knew that this would be a day to remember.

Next she began the lesson with a simple introduction. "Today we will study the story of Goliath and David."

With that blunder, almost everyone in class erupted in the kind of vigorous laughter that boys frequently use to point out adult mistakes. As young as we were, we still knew that the proper title of that battle story is "David and Goliath." No one had ever said it or heard it said or even thought about it as "Goliath and David."

Only I didn't laugh. It wasn't that I was more sensitive than the others. I just didn't get it as quickly. I had to ponder the situation and then have someone explain it to me before I could catch the humor.

So I just sat there and thought about what she had said for a few seconds. But I still didn't laugh, even after thinking about it. I was too intrigued with this new idea. It's one that deserves some attention.

In all my years of envisioning this story, of playing it out in vivid detail through the wonder of my mind's pictures, I had always seen it unfold through David's thoughts and eyes—his pleading to go to battle, struggling against the oversized armor, choosing the right stones, firing the missile, and watching the conquered giant fall in front of him.

But Mrs. Parish, with her trembling slip of tongue, gave my imagining a whole new dimension. There are two characters here—two minds, two sets of eyes, two plans of action. When we ignore Goliath's view in this story, we miss a very important point. From David we learn the lesson of the winner, but from Goliath we learn the lesson of the loser. And that lesson is too important to overlook.

For all we know, Goliath might have been a nice person underneath all his tough-guy exterior. He might have been a loving husband and father. We do know that he was a willing soldier ready to stand up for his leader and army. Of course, he probably didn't believe he was really risking all that much at the time.

But regardless of the kind of person he was, Goliath made one fatal error: he dared to stand up against God. That's the lesson we learn from the loser. Regardless of how tough we think we are, we can't stand up against God.

There have been those who have tried it, and we have accounts of the consequences. Pharaoh tried it, and Jonah, and Herod, and Ananias, and Goliath.

It would seem that from all this evidence that we would somehow manage to master this concept, but I am not sure I've learned it yet in its fullness.

In an attempt at justification, perhaps I could

engage in a deep theological debate about what God wants from me, what His will is, and what the Bible really means, especially in its confusing parts.

But that's a smoke screen. When I finally come around to being honest with myself, I have to confess that I'm not even living out those parts of the Bible that are perfectly clear.

But I do have some help. Every time my memory wanders back to Sunday School days, and I remember Mrs. Parish's contribution to my moral development, I take a peek through Goliath's eyes and see that one stone coming straight for my head. And then I understand that it's always foolhardy to stand up against God.

The Lesson of
A MAN'S TEARS

"REAL MEN don't eat food that begins with the letter Q," the scholars of real men tell us. In fact, those scholars give us a whole list of don'ts for real men.

But at the top of this list of awesome don'ts that separate the macho from the meek, the weighty from the wimps, is the consistent code, "Real men don't cry."

That's the first law of the street. We begin to learn it about the same time we begin to eat with a spoon, and we have the lesson superimposed on our faces and personalities with the frequent repetition required of all good education.

At the height of his teasing, the bully taunts us, "What are you going to do? Cry?" as if crying would be the greatest imaginable display of human weakness.

When the ball hits us during the backyard game and we turn into patches of purple welts, we are constantly being reminded of the code. "Spit on it and play," we are told. "Whatever you do, don't cry."

Even mothers contribute to the cause. During the process of growing up, which for most of us lasts a lifetime, there come those moments when the logical response is just to sit and cry.

One of the fish in the tank dies. Our best friend can't come over, and everybody else doesn't want to come over either. The homework is too hard. When we get to grow the beans in a cup in class, ours are the puniest ones. The Cardinals lose a game.

Mother's function at these moments of tragedy is to come, wipe the tears away with the cleanest corner of her apron, and say, "Now you mustn't cry. Crying won't make it any better."

And from this, we learn early and know forever that real men don't cry.

David was a real man. We learned that in Sunday School once. In fact, we learned that in Sunday School one whole quarter.

We knew that quarter was going to be special the moment we saw the new Sunday School book. On the front cover was the picture of this gigantic man dressed in full armor, swinging a spiky ball around his head and sneering ferociously at this innocent looking boy standing in front of him holding a homemade slingshot. The picture itself told the story of valor, preparedness, innocence, and the unreasonableness of faith. Who could resist such an appeal?

The lessons inside only accented the theme. David was indeed a real man. He ate the right foods, he camped out in the wilderness, he was loyal to his friends, and he fought the enemy in the face of great odds.

In short, David became my hero. He was the kind of man I wished I could be. I think that's what having a hero means to all of us. In those places in our hearts where God is the only outsider allowed to visit, we wish we were the hero.

Most of us tell ourselves that we actually wish for the circumstances of heroism. We dream of that moment when we face the sneering, armed giant and attack with nothing but initiative and a smooth rock. We dream on of applause and accolades and honor that would surely come to us — if only we had the opportunity.

But the truth is, it isn't just opportunity that we lack. When the giant comes — and there are more giants in life than we often recognize — most of us are probably lurking way back in the foxholes somewhere sniveling with the rest of Saul's army.

But David was a real man. He stepped forward and fought the giant.

One day, Mrs. Murphy started the lesson by writing on the board in big letters, FRIENDSHIP, and we spent the whole hour imagining David and Jonathan running around the wilderness, hiding from Saul, sharing secrets and being buddies.

That's the stuff of real men too — having real buddies. Real men have buddies who require sneaking and thigh-slapping and loyalty.

But just about the time the bell was to ring, signaling the end of intentional learning, the beginning of socially inspired incidental learning, and peace to Mrs. Murphy, we hurried through those last few verses, crowding everything in to avoid the cardinal sin of omitting something important enough to be published in the quarterly.

It was Jerry Hill's time to read and he read fast like he was in a game of Hot Potato and didn't want to be "It" when the bell rang.

"After the boy had gone, David got up from the south side of the stone and bowed down before Jonathan three times with his face to the ground. Then they kissed each other and wept together — but David wept the most," he panted vocally at the end, proud that he had made it all the way through.

But even in the rush of the singsong reading, and the shuffling of a class of boys gathering their possessions, and the continued activity of such distractions, at the two-minute warning, I caught those last words, "But David wept the most."

Those words stabbed into my being with the cold piercing sharpness of a frozen knife. I wanted to cry out. I wanted commentary, explanation, or at least solace.

But the bell rang, and I lost not only teaching but companionship. I sat back down in the classroom all alone, and stared at that one word staring back at me from the board, FRIENDSHIP. And I thought and I thought. I thought until my brother came to find me and chide me for making him late to worship service again.

He stood at the door and rebuked. But I had to know the meaning of all this, and my brother was infinitely wise, being five years older than I.

I asked, "Do real men cry?"

"Of course not, Dummy," he answered with sibling cordiality, "but I'm going to make you cry if you don't come on."

"Was David a real man?" I asked again quietly.

"Sure! He whipped Goliath. Hurry up," he spoke from wisdom.

"But David wept the most?" The words came from and through the heart and mouth in such a way that the sentence became an interrogative instead of declarative. "How do you explain that?"

"There is a difference between weeping and crying," my brother said, just before he grabbed my ear and led me away.

I heard and I followed, and I thought about what he said, but I still think he's wrong.

The Lesson of
THE FIRST AND LAST

SOME BIBLE LESSONS are straightforward and blunt. Some Bible lessons are reminding and gentle. Some Bible lessons are refreshing and inspiring. And some Bible lessons are just plain tough. Not only are they difficult to apply, but just about the time you think you are beginning to know what the lesson has to say to the way you live, you sort of start wishing the Bible didn't say that at all.

Personally, I have always had trouble with Christ's promise or admonition—I can't really tell which—that the first shall be last and the last shall be first. I have heard the preachers exhort; I have read the commentaries; and I have even heard the televangelists proclaim. But I must confess that I'm still not really sure I understand all of what I am supposed to make with that piece of truth.

Nevertheless, I do have an illustration. In our Sunday School, we had two very different families—the Smiths and the Hendersons. The Smiths were always the first ones there. I am not sure I know how early they came because they had already arrived, turned up the heat, pulled the thistles away from the doors, settled in, dusted the piano, and drawn pictures on the chalkboard by the time anyone else got there. This wasn't just once; they did it every Sunday that I can remember. When my memory returns to boyhood and the joy of Sunday School, the first memory of all is walking into the building and being greeted by the Smiths. Because they got there first, they had their choice of all the seats in the house, so each one sat in the very same seat every Sunday with a sense of ownership.

The Smiths knew this about themselves and wore their early arrival like a badge of honor. It was their contribution to the Sunday School and to its legend. I think that if some other family had ventured out as early as the Smiths did, they would have probably stopped along the road somewhere just so the Smiths could keep their streak in tact.

On the other hand, we had the Hendersons. Just as the Smiths were always first, the Hendersons were always the last to arrive. They would come straggling in halfway through the song service, struggling with buttoning their shirts and tying their Sunday School Shoes. Mrs. Smith would occasionally even change the order of service so that we would pray after the Hendersons got there. Since the Hendersons were always late, they always had to take the last vacant seats. My memories of Sunday School include those images of the Hendersons tromping past seated people to get to vacant chairs.

The Hendersons knew this about themselves and wore their late arrival like a badge of honor.

The Smiths lived way back on the other side of the big hills, and were the only family that came from beyond those hills. In fact, the Smiths lived farther away than any other family, and the roads were bad out there.

The Hendersons lived next to the church. In fact, their yard butted up against the church lawn, and they had a path worn where they cut through every Sunday—not more than a hundred feet away by the shortcut.

I don't know how this applies to what Jesus taught us, but I do enjoy remembering it, and I think there may be a subtle message about human nature and even the Christian journey. Sometimes, the people with the farthest to go get there first.

The Lesson of
THE MEMORABLE PART

THE BIG EVENT each year was Sunday School Rally Day. This is the day we gave the whole Sunday service to things like teacher recognition and promotions and a big program. Rally Day drew the biggest attendance of the year. Maybe people came because all the children had a speaking part. On the other hand, maybe they came because the preacher didn't have much of a speaking part.

The purpose of the day seemed to be to showcase talent and training. We recited the Bible verses we had learned, sang the songs we had prepared just for the event, gave an exhibition Sword Drill, and staged a play with memorized lines and everything.

The play was a big deal, and the assignment of

parts was a major test of social science insight and theatrically educated hunches. Our Sunday School world was divided into two kinds of people—those who wanted a part in the play and weren't ashamed to admit it, and those who wanted a part in the play but were too embarrassed to show it. Mrs. Smith, who assigned the parts, seemed to understand that. Sometimes she would give the biggest part to the person who protested the most about even being in "a sissy old play" much less starring in it. But this was always the person who beamed the most when we took the curtain call.

One year we staged the Parable of the Prodigal Son. Mrs. Smith wrote the play herself, so she understood it well, and she understood us too. Since there were two party scenes, she had minor parts for almost everybody, and she assigned those first.

The rest stood around waiting with great anticipation and feigned apprehension. Some kids had even read ahead and knew what the choice parts were. Roger Mahoney was given the part of the older brother because, as Mrs. Smith explained, he had the personality for it. And since Roger hadn't read ahead, he thought that was a compliment. Then Mrs. Smith assigned the younger brother and even the father to the logical choices, and we all nodded agreement with her expertise.

And finally everybody had a part, except Dennis Jarvis, the chubby kid in our class. He might have been a nice person deep down inside, but nobody would ever know that because everybody picked on him so much that he had to be ornery in self-defense. Dennis didn't really stutter, but he talked so fast that he had to back up once in a while to get in the syllables he had left out the first time through.

And when he didn't have a part, we wondered if maybe Mrs. Smith had forgotten, but we wondered only a moment. In her typical ability to make the simple sound important, Mrs. Smith explained that she had saved the best part of all for Dennis. He would play the role of the fattened calf. Even though we wanted to laugh, we didn't until Dennis laughed. He enjoyed the role.

On Sunday School Rally Day, Dennis played his role to the maximum. He made a costume by putting a paper bag over his head and wearing a set of construction paper horns. He came on stage walking on all fours, and he bellowed and stomped just like a real calf. And the congregation laughed their appreciation.

When it was all over and we took the curtain call, Dennis got the biggest and wildest applause, even bigger than Roger Mahoney got for playing the older brother, and he had the personality for the part.

I had the opportunity to visit my old home church a couple of years ago. Although it had been forty years, the place looked just the same, only smaller, and the memories wiped forty years of wrinkles off my face and heart just for a moment.

That day I met an older man who would have been in the audience when we portrayed the story of the Prodigal Son on that Sunday School Rally Day.

He helped me remember, and his recalling powers were good, except that he kept running generations together and told me about people who were at least seven years older or seven years younger than I, as if they were my peer group.

Finally, there came a time in the conversation when it seemed appropriate to ask about Dennis Jarvis. I realized there was a risk involved since Dennis was not particularly the memorable type. But as soon as I breathed his name, the older gent grinned a beacon of recognition and exclaimed in full appreciation, "Oh, you mean the kid who played the fattened calf?"

Throughout Hollywood, throughout Broadway, throughout all of India, there are men and women who make their living at acting who could only wish for what Dennis accomplished on that make-shift stage while wearing a paper sack over his head. He created a role that would live in the memories and hearts of those who saw him.

To make this a better story, I would tell you that Dennis is now a successful business executive. But the man I was talking with didn't know where Dennis was. And neither do I. But that doesn't matter. Dennis still had his moment of greatness.

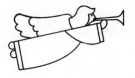

The Lesson of
THE TALENTS

IN SUNDAY SCHOOL I learned the lesson of the talents. Maybe I should say I learned the lessons of the talents because, as is often the case, there are at least two lessons here. There is the lesson they teach you in class and the lesson you learn just hanging around paying attention.

The lesson we learned in class was noteworthy enough. We actually covered this section of the Gospel of Matthew during Mrs. Murphy's flannelgraph story.

Dedicated teacher that she was, she went so far as to make herself an apron covered with the flannelgraph stickum stuff so that as the lesson unfolded she could slap those scenes up on her chest with both hands. It was almost as good as the Saturday afternoon Western down at the Rialto Movie House.

On the morning of the lessons of the talents, the scenes and images manipulated by her dextrous fingers literally flew by and stuck permanently in our impressionable minds made even more impressionable through the use of the sense of seeing as well as hearing.

First we learned all about the guy with five talents, about his busyness and hard work and business acumen. But most of all, we learned about happiness. Mrs. Murphy didn't mention it because she didn't have to. It was presented in vivid color across her chest. That man smiled when he received the talents. He smiled as he worked, and everybody smiled during the reunion when his master came back.

The story was about the same for the fellow with two talents; but when we saw the man with only one talent, the whole tone changed. From the beginning, you could see that this was a person afraid. He looked sad while he received the talent; but more than sad, he seemed to be filled with feelings of suspicion. He had that look about him that Roger Brady had the day he brought Life Savers to Sunday School and tried to eat them without being caught by the teachers, or by other kids who would have demanded that he share.

The reunion for the one-talent man was especially sad. The master was harsh and the man was dejected and went off and cowered in a corner.

That's the story we saw in class, and its lesson was just as powerful. We learned that we should all use our talents regardless of what they were. We also learned that some of us had been given five talents, some had been given two talents and some of us had only one.

As dutiful children in Sunday School, we all sat and agreed with that principle because we already knew who among us were cute, who could sing, who could play ball, and who got the biggest part in the Rally Day program. We knew about the rationing of talents.

But I learned another lesson of talents by watching the Sunday School administration. Mrs. Smith was the person in charge of the little kids' section, and she was good. In fact, she was about the best-liked person in all of the church.

Because of that, they made her Superintendent over the whole Sunday School. After that, nobody liked her much. The change in status came from her position and not from her personality.

As best as I can tell, the Sunday School Superintendent's biggest job is to find somebody to act as teacher in every class. As best as I can tell, there are two kinds of teaching appointments. There are life-time appointments and panic appointments. In other words, there are those teachers who come from the womb with a Scripture Press Quarterly in one hand and a box of broken crayons in the other. These are the Lifers. They are born to teach.

On the other hand, there are those teachers who are pressed into the corps from the panic caused by the thought of half-crazed junior high youth running loose in a small room with no adult supervision. They are forced into teaching because of this inherent panic, and they respond with the same kind of emotion.

As best as I can tell, the secret to good Sunday School management is to keep the Lifers and the Panickers apart. The Lifers are always telling us of things like dedication and devotion. "I always begin my lesson preparation on Sunday afternoon a full week ahead," they explain to the rest of us. "That way, I can have the whole week to search the commentaries, brush up on the Greek verbs, and create my own flannelgraph materials."

Do you have any idea what that kind of talk does to a person already pressing against multiple layers of panic and wondering if there is enough time on Saturday night to scan a text?

Well, this is the problem Superintendent Smith confronted, and it helped me understand how we all feel about the Parable of the Talents — not how we feel theologically but practically. Nothing brings out my appreciation of that text as effectively as asking a reluctant prospect to teach the sixth grade boys.

Except for those Lifers, most folks don't really believe they have more than one talent, and they repel all invitations to serve, not because they are lazy, but because they are trying to be realistic. And they may be close to accurate.

As best as I can tell, most of us do expect our teachers to have the encouraging ability of a Barnabas, the exegetical skill of a Paul, the story-telling gift of a Nathan, the musical talent of a David, and the work ethic of a Martha. And one-talented people need not apply.

That's the lesson I learned from Mrs. Smith.

# The Lesson of
FINGER LICKING

I ALWAYS LIKED the game of Sword Drill because it reminded me of basketball. It was fast-paced, and the action came in spurts sprinkled throughout large blocks of anticipation time. Success depended on an unusual combination of skill and accident, and to the uneducated eye, it all looked disorganized, just like basketball.

But I liked Sword Drill better than basketball because I was good at Sword Drill. I was almost the best. Actually, I was second best. The only person I couldn't beat was Mary Alice Bickford, and that was disheartening. I dreaded going up against her. My stomach would knot up, and I would make my head hurt from squinting my eyes so I could concentrate on the text and my cognitive map of the Bible as I waited for Mrs. Smith to say, "All ready. . . . Charge!"

At that command, I would tear into my Bible as fast as I could, working my fingers through the pages and flipping and turning, and just as I was no more than two chapters away, Mary Alice would start to read, and I was beat again.

It wasn't just a matter of getting beat that was so painful, but it was getting beat by Mary Alice. When she won, she didn't gloat, and that made it bad. People are always saying how they love a gracious winner; but frankly, I don't much appreciate a gracious winner when the person they beat to get there is me.

The bad thing about Mary Alice's attitude is that she didn't gloat, she didn't boast, and she didn't act modest either. She just stood there about as unemotional as a person ought to be after she has just knocked off the whole children's Sunday School department for Sword Drill Championship of the Western World. The thing that bothered me most was she didn't even look surprised that she had beat me. She just looked as if this was what she intended to do in the first place.

I have been around sports enough to know that at the times in your life when you are only second best, and really want to be first best, you have two options. You can learn to cheat or you can practice. I opted for the second option. I practiced. I worked hard. I did finger exercises. I carried a tennis ball in my pocket and squeezed it to build up wrist muscles. I sat up late at night and wrote the books of the Bible in order. Then when I had mastered that, I practiced holding entire books in my right hand so that I would recognize just what the Book of Proverbs felt like between the finger and the thumb.

I even went so far as to add a few strategic dog-ears at the beginning of such sections as the minor prophets.

In short, I was prepared for the next Sword Drill battle. Again, I drew Mary Alice, and because this was the championship set, we had to go the best three out of five rounds. The first command was Romans 8:29, and I was only two verses away when Mary Alice began to read, and then she stood there looking not surprised.

Down but not out, I stuck a Life Saver in my

mouth for the quick energy I would need for the second round. This time it was Exodus 48:2, and I was right there. I even had my finger on the very verse itself, and Mary Alice started to read.

Down the opening two, I lost all hope. I didn't tell anybody, and I tried to look confident, but I was lying. I knew I wasn't going to win. I knew that I would have to spend the rest of my life being second best. When Mrs. Smith gave the text and she called the charge, I didn't even open my Bible. Instead, I turned to watch Mary Alice. And that's when I learned her secret. She licked her fingers. Just when Mrs. Smith cried, "Charge," Mary Alice licked her fingers.

That's what I learned from Sunday School Sword Drill and Mary Alice Bickford. And it is one of the most important lessons I mastered during those growing years.

I hear you scoff. "How can such a thing as learning to lick your fingers before you flip through the Bible be so consequential?" you ask.

But this lesson has immediate application. Many a time on Sunday morning, this little piece of simple knowledge has turned a potentially confusing situation into a significant spiritual experience.

For one thing, during the morning worship service, I always sit as far away from the preacher as I can get. This practice has some obvious advantages, but there is one distinct disadvantage. It takes sound a lot longer to travel back to where I am. How often the preacher enjoys giving the Scripture text in crescendo. He begins, "Today, we are going to read about times like now. Today, we will read words that are just as relevant as they were when they were written thousands of years ago. Today, we will read of a man who speaks the word of God." Meanwhile, the pitch and pace are rising, and I sit with the Bible poised and the anticipation of a Sword Drill charge to follow. Then he says, "Today, we will read from (long pause) Obadiah chapter two." Then he breathes a short breath and starts to read, thinking that everybody in the congregation is following along word for word.

There is, of course, an important preaching principle applied here. Preachers are taught this in seminary, and even those who make bad grades master it well. The more obscure the passage, the

143

less time you give the congregation to look for it.

But I am on top of this—with Sword Drill experience and my piece of knowledge. I just lick my fingers and get there.

But even beyond this, this little lesson has metaphorical application as well. How often we tell ourselves that a task is too tough for us. How often we begin to accept ourselves as second best. How often we talk ourselves out of trying. And all the time, the secret is as simple as licking your fingers. What a philosopher that Mary Alice Bickford was!

Just the other day, one of my bosses called me into his office. He had been away to an important seminar on people management and other such learned skills, and he wanted to practice his new lessons in an attempt to justify the money he had spent.

He moved out from behind his desk and sat just across from me looking me straight in the eyes. He unfolded his arms and uncrossed his legs and looked as if he were truly open to my suggestions.

He bent over and closed the distance between us, and in a tone that sounded as if he had a significant institutional secret which we had to protect with our lives, he said, "Cliff, there's a difference between working hard and working smart." He leaned back and took the posture and tone that said that he was satisfied with himself for having revealed that to me, and he said, "Do know what I mean?"

"Yes," I answered. "I think I do. It's like Mary Alice Bickford licking her fingers in Sword Drill."

I don't need the seminars. I've been to Sunday School.

The Lesson of JOHN 3:16

PROGRESS is more than jumping at whatever is new. It is also diligently clinging to what worked in the past.

Mrs. Murphy was a progressive teacher. She used flannelgraph before some of the others had even settled the question of whether it was theologically sound. She used a tape recorder even before there were cassettes. She made copies before mimeographs, when she had to print sheet by sheet with a rolling pin and a pan of jelly. And she gave us Life Savers for getting the answers right.

Yet, Mrs. Murphy clung diligently to what was sound in the past. In other words, she believed in Bible memorization. She not only believed in Bible memorization as a teaching tool, but she had even memorized major sections herself. That's how much she believed in it.

Every Sunday, she would start the class by standing in front of us and reciting some significant portion. But with Mrs. Murphy Bible memorization and recitation was different. Some people seem to memorize Scripture for the same reason that other people take cold showers. If they didn't do it, they wouldn't have anything else to brag about.

But during Mrs. Murphy's recital, we students got the idea that this was important for other reasons. With her it seemed significant, a crucial step in her spiritual walk; and even on those frequent occasions when we students didn't fully grasp all the content, we still listened in the kind of awed silence that children are trapped into involuntarily on those rare times when they are genuinely impressed.

In recent years when such things as children and Sunday Schools are being visited by calculator-carrying social scientists, the teaching/learning technique of Bible memorization has fallen on some rough times. Of course, I'm not much of a scientist but only a reminiscer, and I don't want to dispute their work. But I do enjoy remembering Mrs. Murphy recite, and I hope my granddaughter will someday enjoy the same kind of moment.

Mrs. Murphy not only memorized herself, but she turned us into memorizers as well. She made it an assignment, and we did it. I am not sure I remember why. There weren't any grades in Sunday School, so that wasn't a factor. We didn't have telephones, so she couldn't threaten to call our parents. Just getting one Life Saver a Sunday wasn't enough of a bribe to hold us to task during the whole week it took to memorize. Maybe we worked at our memorization because we liked the way Mrs. Murphy did it.

I shall never forget the Sunday we started. She introduced the class with a long recitation of a Psalm, and we listened as intently as if David himself were singing. Then she stopped and said, "Next week, it will be your turn," and we stared at each other in feigned fear.

"You will memorize one verse and recite it for the class next Sunday," she continued the assignment.

149

We responded with the standard protests that are required by the Laws of International Studentship anytime any assignment is given.

"We've never ever done this before."

"Does the other class have to do it?"

"Can we put it off a week?"

"This is dumb."

She stood her ground, and we surrendered easily, mostly because we knew it would be exciting.

But after she had persuaded us that we would do the assignment, we had to get a clarity in the directions. This is also required by the Laws of International Studentship.

"Does it have to be a whole verse?"

"Can it be more than one verse?"

"If we memorize two verses, can we use one for the Sunday after?"

"Can we memorize a verse from the New Testament?"

"Can we memorize a verse from the Old Testament?"

"Can we memorize a verse from the concordance?"

"What is a verse?"

Once we had exhausted the list of requisite questions, a sort of positive anxiousness fell on the room. It seemed that we all wanted to get into it. I told you that Mrs. Murphy was a progressive teacher.

That afternoon, while most of the family was napping, I borrowed my mom's Bible to begin preparation. At that time I didn't know much about what was in that rather austere looking black book. I had begun to read it once from the beginning, but I hadn't really made it out of the Garden of Eden yet. The only other thing I knew about it was those words and phrases that sort of hopped off the page while I was flipping through enroute to the beginning, and the most impressive one of those was something named Selah.

But this day was different. I would have to recite what I had learned, so I needed to search for the right verse. This was more than an exercise of personal memorization. This was also our introduction to Christian witnessing.

Some of my mom's Bible was printed in red; and being the strategist that I was, I reasoned that what was in red must be the most important. I would go for something in red. So I plopped the Bible down, and it sort of fell open to this particular spot as if it had a mind of its own. From my own personal experience and hearing other people talk, I think Bibles do this occasionally.

With my finger, I touched one of the red verses and read, "For God so loved the world that He gave His only begotten Son that whosoever believeth in Him should not perish, but have everlasting life."

From that moment on, I have known what it is to discover gold. I didn't know all the words, and I had trouble pronouncing what I did know. But that didn't matter. I knew enough to recognize that this was truth. Here was what I needed to know. Here was soothing water for the burning from my boyish fears. I read it over and over and over. I began to memorize, and the task was easy. The words seemed to stick in my brain. In that one short session, I mastered the memorization.

But that wasn't enough. I practiced all week. I said it to the cows while I milked. I said it to the hogs as I poured slop first in the small trough and then in the big one. In class, I said it under my breath between the schoolwork. "7 x 9 is 63 For God so loved the world 8 x 7 is 56 that He gave His only Son—that He gave His only begotten Son 6 x 7 is..."

After about two months of that, next Sunday came and brought with it my big opportunity.

The verse was so powerful and I could say it so well that I just knew that I would be an instant hit in the whole class.

When it came time to volunteer for reciting order, I thought about holding my hand up quickly like kids do when they demand to be first, but I realized that would be too obvious. Instead I hung in the background and waited until I was assigned fifth. That was a good spot. I would wait with that opossum look as if they were all better than I; then I would spring it on them right in the middle.

Bobby Lee Stockton was first, and after some required protests about position and posture (more Laws of International Studentship), he moved to the front, grinned a bit, and said, "For God so loved the world that He gave His only begotten Son, that whosoever believeth in Him should not perish, but have everlasting life." To

153

make it even worse, he said it perfectly.

I was stunned. That Bible is full of verses, more than people can even count, so why did he pick that one? Besides, that verse had jumped out at me as if it were my very own. And now here was my verse in the mouth of somebody else. I was not only stunned, but I felt a little betrayed.

If I showed it, Mrs. Murphy either didn't notice or was gracious enough to act as if she didn't, so we went on to Roger Goodner who was second.

He stood, grinned, and said, "For God so loved the world that He gave His only begotten Son . . ."

To make a long story short (if it's not too late already), six of the eight had memorized John 3:16, and the other two had discovered the delight of "Jesus wept."

Now, you may think that this day was one of the blue letter disappointment days of my life. But no day is a disappointment if it has pleasant consequences, and this day has proven to be one of my great moments.

Of course, I learned shortly after that this whole thing was a put-up job. Those kids had all memorized John 3:16 for Vacation Bible School the summer before, and they were just taking the easy way out.

But that still doesn't deter from the awesome and comprehensive content of the verse. In fact, it adds to it. Because of the sequence of events that day, I have learned something really important about John 3:16. It is my very own verse that God gave specially to me. But He also gave it to a lot of other people for their special verse too — Bobby Lee Stockton and Roger Goodner and that person who goes to football games and holds up the sign when the television cameras are focused on the end zone.

It belongs to each one of us specially, and to all of us specially. And that makes us a family.

Sometimes I get caught in those situations when I just can't get to my Bible for devotions that day. So I say John 3:16, refresh my soul, and remember practicing it to the cows.

Sometimes I try to pray, and my mouth spits out brain dust instead. So I say John 3:16, refresh my soul, and remember practicing it to the hogs.

Sometimes I become God's agent in inviting and welcoming new members into the family. So I say

John 3:16, refresh my soul, and tell them the Sunday School story, partly to break the ice, and partly because I want them to memorize it too.

I think I know how Mrs. Murphy must have felt that day.

The Lesson of
THE NEW BOOK

I FEEL SORRY for people who don't go to Sunday School. That's one place where the Bible lesson refreshes us with promise and challenge, where the fellowship reminds us that we are not alone, and where the food at the carry-in dinner is memorable.

Those are the obvious good times, but there are some subtle good times that are just as delightful.

Personally, I look forward to the day we get new Sunday School books. Isn't this wonderful? For those regulars in Sunday School, we always have this big day of anticipation just ahead. It's like being a student and living in a state of expectancy until the last day of school. It's even better because it comes once every three months.

When I was a child and life had not yet become burdened with too many books, that day of the new Sunday School book was one of the major events of my life. Back then the volume was called the Quarterly, and it was more than a mere collection of lessons for the next three months. With a cover adorned with a picture appropriate for the season, the Quarterly was a symbol of progress — maybe not the progress of the species, but at least of the individual. The new Quarterly told us that the past was over and that there was an excitement on the road yet in front of us.

In our little Sunday School, Mrs. Smith was in charge of the distribution. The big moment came at the very conclusion of opening exercises. As the creed required, we would sing, listen to an introduction to the lesson, collect the birthday offering, and pray. Usually, upon pronouncement of the Amen, we would all make a mad dash to our own little corner room and fight for available chairs. But on the special day of the new Quarterly, we didn't break away. We stood in boy reverence — which is not to be confused with real reverence, and waited with boy patience — which is not to be confused with real patience, as Mrs. Smith moved among us, diligently and tenderly handing each person a new book which contained the joy and the hope of the next three months. It was a big moment, even for those who never studied; and it was always the kind of moment which made you glad that you came to Sunday School and made you especially happy that you had come this particular day.

That's the way it was during my boyhood days in the valley, and that's the way it still is for me. But getting a new book is more than just another Red Letter Day in our lives. There seems to be an important lesson here. On the other hand, maybe there isn't any lesson at all; but through my years as a teacher facing the charge of filling a full hour every Sunday morning with something valuable, I have learned to spot lessons even in those places where none exist.

Nevertheless, I would like to think I can find at least one lesson lurking in the ritual of getting new books, and that is the lesson of timing.

When we first get the new books, they literally glow with newness. They feel new. They smell new. The colors are brillant; the type is bold and readable; and the pages lie flat.

But during three months of use, wear takes a toll. The colors in the pictures smudge. The type fades. Fingerprints cover essential concepts, and coffee stains blot out hundreds of years of Hebrew history. Those pages which aren't dog-eared curl up so that you either have to study the lesson with an iron on hand or bend your neck to read words on a curve.

Just as you think nothing else could go wrong, the staples back out and twenty-seven percent of the pages fly loose in your hand.

At least, that's the way my lesson book looks. I notice that other people in class have better preserved models, but I just tell myself that they don't study as much as I do. Still, I have to wonder why they can answer more questions.

But there is always hope. On that very Sunday when you have to gather up the remains from all corners of the house and know that you can't go through this one more time, you get a new book and start all over. This is the excitement of timing.

About the time the old book completely disintegrates, we get a new one.

About the time our lap begins to spread, we get grandchildren to fill the extra space.

About the time we have so much arthritis in our hands that we can't floss, our teeth fall out.

About the time we lose all confidence in the human race, the harried woman in front of us with a whole cart of groceries steps aside and lets us go first through the checkout line.

When the time is right, Jesus will come again.

Now, I realize that there is a pretty huge theological chasm between the idea of worn-out lesson books and Christ's coming. Nevertheless, there seems to be a powerful underlying thought at work here.

God is in charge of the dimension of time. That's good to know. No, that's *great* to know. In one of his letters, Paul got so excited about that little piece of factual information that every time he thought about it, he would stop and say, "Now encourage one another." In other words, living our lives in constant and operational knowledge that God is in charge of time is about the most encouraging thought we can ever have.

Bookstores are filled with volumes which tell us how to think positively and behave as if we think positively. Maybe we just need to remember that God is in charge of time.

But remembering this is tough because it requires the practice of patience. We often talk of patience as if it is a good thing to have. We even pray for patience. But we pray impatiently.

When I was a teenager, I prayed for a pickup truck. In those days, a pickup truck was the symbol of manliness, rugged individualism, and freedom.

I didn't want just any pickup truck. I wanted a pickup truck with outside mirrors, a gun rack, and a big dog policing the back, riding along with his face in the wind.

I prayed vigorously. I prayed impatiently. After a while when I didn't get a pickup truck, I quit praying.

Thirty years later, after I had grown out of being a teenager and had matured into manhood, I got a pickup truck. But by this time, it was a symbol of service. I could help people move, help clean up garbage, and haul the tables around for the church social—just another reminder that God is in charge of timing.

Every three months, I enjoy getting my new Sunday School book. I like the way it feels in my hands. But I particularly enjoy remembering to pray for patience.

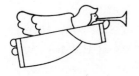 *The Lesson of*
"AND LO"

CHRISTMAS AND SUNDAY SCHOOL go together. Like ham and eggs, bread and butter, and Mutt and Jeff, the words blend into one image and one memory. I'm not sure how people who didn't grow up in Sunday School celebrate the Christmas season, but they have to be missing something.

Without Sunday School, how would you even know that Christmas was coming, and that it was time to start building good will and anticipation?

For us, the harbinger, the first hint, was the assigning of parts. Some Sunday morning, before anyone quite expected it, Mrs. Smith would announce in opening exercises, "Today we must begin to work on the Christmas program."

Next she would distribute parts. From those handwritten sheets with our names at the top, we got the idea that Mrs. Smith had stayed awake way into the night for several nights just thinking about each one of us and what we could do special to help our whole church see Christ in Christmas.

Then she would call on the kid with part One, and he would read, "There were in the same country shepherds abiding in their fields, keeping watch over their flocks by night. And lo, the angel of the Lord came upon them, and the glory of the Lord shone round about them; and they were sore afraid." And with that the Christmas season officially began in our valley.

In later years as I have become more metropolitan in my outlook, living in a town with a traffic light, I have often been amused by the attempts of merchants to announce the Christmas season. They decorate their windows in red, string banners across main street, hire Santa Claus to do television commercials, stuff Sunday papers full of slick pages, and give out calendars.

But I have a better idea. I think it would be simpler and more definite if they could find some kid with boyish cracks in his voice and optimism in his volume to read over a giant loudspeaker, "There were in the same country, shepherds abiding in their fields." Then the world would know that at that instant we should begin the celebration.

To this day, Luke 2 is still a very special spot in my Bible. I don't read it casually or carelessly or too often. Even when I'm reading through the good doctor's Gospel from cover to cover, I skip that part, and wait until that particular day.

You know the day. It comes in July or August. It is that day when the problems rain down like hailstones and pelt you, making your ears and spirit sag. But you see through the problems to a clear and reasonable solution and yet, no one else in the world can see the solution, and so you stand alone. That's what is called a bad day. In the bright sun, there is no light. In the heat, there is no warmth. In the land of promise, there is no hope. Then I read Luke 2: "There were in the same country shepherds abiding in their fields, keeping watch over their flock by night. And lo, the angel of the Lord came upon them." And

Christmas comes to my soul again.

Luke 2 is more than a passage to be read. It is to be partaken by all the senses. It even has its own fragrance — the smell of cedar and cinnamon.

Even in the beginning for me, those words carried significance, but I must confess that I didn't understand them all. From the process of contextualization (I love that word), I figured out the meaning of "abiding" by myself. But for the life of me, I could not decipher the word "lo."

Rather than looking it up in the dictionary which would have been the simple way out, I consulted a sage. I asked my brother. Because he was five years older than I was, he was the living expert on every human matter.

One night during that time of year when we fought each other for covers and visions of chocolate covered cherries danced in our heads, I asked him, "What is lo?"

"What?"

"What is lo?"

"It's underneath," the man of wisdom explained.

"No, it isn't." I was impatient. "It's in the Bible."

"Where?" he said in tones that frustrated me that he wasn't thinking about this too.

"In the Christmas story," I told him. "And lo, the angel of the Lord came upon them."

"Oh, that. Lo is the sound the sheep make," he said rather nonchalantly and went off to sleep.

For the next five years, I spent the Christmas season being a little upset that nobody went "Lo, lo, lo" during the Nativity part of the Sunday School program.

Those Sunday School Christmas programs were major parts of our lives. They were even bigger than Rally Day programs. On Rally Day the people came from all over the community, and we had a big crowd. For the Christmas program, they not only came from all over the community but they brought their kinfolks from California and other exotic places from far-off distances, and we had a gigantic crowd, and cosmopolitan too.

Seeing it all in retrospect, which is an educational way to see it, I realize that those programs served a valuable function in our celebration of Christmas because they gave the whole season a sense of structure and purpose. We had to learn our parts. We had to overcome our fears of performing in public. We had to share ourselves. We had to give something of ourselves. Because of the Christmas program, we couldn't go into the season with hearts of selfishness and greed.

Perhaps it seems like a small gesture now, but giving ourselves to the Christmas program was at least a form of giving. At one time in one generation, there were fourteen children in that little country church who performed in the programs and gave themselves in a small way.

Now thirty years later, each one is serving God, either as a leader in the church world or as a leader in a local church. Somewhere they learned something good.

Not only does Christmas have a definite beginning moment from the world of a Sunday School memory, but it has just as definite a conclusion point as well. Christmas is officially over when you eat the last pecan.

That image comes out of the second great feature of the Sunday School Christmas celebration — The Tradition of the Sack.

We didn't give away treats or toys or even bags.

We gave sacks. At the conclusion of the Christmas program, after the final chorus of "Silent Night" and the bow-taking, and the grinning sheepishly among the feelings of "I knew I would be the star," we all sat down, and the men of the church came up and handed out "the sacks."

We lived for the sacks. This was one of the great anticipation points of the winter season. They were filled with all sorts of good things, an orange and an apple, chocolates, hard candy, orange candy slices, peanuts and pecans.

Things like the orange slices and chocolates went fast. The hard candy was put into storage to be savored on long winter nights when you had to do chores after dark. Since the peanuts required both hands and couldn't be eaten with gloves on, we saved those for the evenings when we were reading in our bedrooms.

But the pecans were the biggest challenge. They were almost seductively delicious, but eating them required singleness of purpose. We didn't have a nutcracker, so the only way to achieve the joy of the taste was to mash two of them together in our hands. It was a slow process, but worth the effort.

About two weeks later when the sack was only a dim recollection and good will was beginning to wane, we would be rummaging through the sofa cushions and would discover that one lone pecan that had been dropped in our haste when the sack was still full and our hearts were light.

Since we didn't have but one, we had nothing to mash it against, so we would bash it with our shoe and eat so slowly, making the memory last and last and last until once more some kid would stand up in Sunday School and read, "There were in the same country shepherds abiding in their fields keeping watch over their flocks by night. And lo, the angel of the Lord came upon them, and the glory of the Lord shone round about them; and they were sore afraid."

The Lesson of
THE FOUR COLORS

ONE MAJOR PROBLEM in the world is that we don't listen enough to little children. We jest about something called "out of the mouths of babes," and we all know a story or two about how a young person spoke some pertinent insight that set the situation straight. But most of the time, we dismiss what children say and do as just so much child's play. Once in awhile I realize how really shortsighted that is.

Not long ago I had to visit a school because the administration wanted to talk with me about their problems. There was unrest among the faculty. Funds were in short supply. Everywhere I go anymore, money seems to be one of the problems, and as I examine matters more closely, often it becomes The Problem. In addition to all these problems, in this school, parents were upset and were protesting various affairs and situations. And I was going to the school to work as a mediator. Needless to say, this didn't have the promise of being a wonderful afternoon.

As I walked across the playground on my way to the battleground, I passed by a group of young girls who were involved in a rather advanced stage of jump rope. This group of children was what some would call a rainbow coalition. It appeared that the only requirement of membership was to be rather accomplished at jumping.

Walking by as casually as I could so I wouldn't seem too conspicuous while fighting the urge to linger and appreciate, I had just enough time to catch the tune they were singing to keep time with the swinging and jumping. I recognized it as something familiar, something I had known from somewhere, but since I didn't have time to hear the words and since they were all singing out of breath anyway, I dismissed this unidentified tune and made my way to the more important meeting.

But as the afternoon and the conversation wore

on, and I wore out, I caught myself mentally humming the tune I had picked up from the girls. It was familiar and pleasant and something from my past; in spite of everything else going on in the room at that time, that tune kept fighting its way to the front of my consciousness.

Since I can't see my own face at times like these, I have no idea how I must have looked to the others sitting around the table; but there I sat listening as best as I could with one ear and humming that old tune in my heart.

About midafternoon, I began to piece the words in their appropriate places in the tune. At first, I just fitted the words instead of a hum here or there and didn't even think or even remember the connection. But suddenly it came to me and I remembered the song and the circumstances.

> Jesus loves the little children,
> All the children of the world.
> Red and yellow, black and white,
> They are precious in His sight,
> Jesus loves the little children of the world.

When the words came to me, my memories jumped back to those Sunday School days so many years ago when we sang this song heartily and meant it. At the time in our valley, we didn't know that much about all four colors. We knew about white, but as yet we hadn't had a lot of experience with red, yellow, or black; so when we sang, the emphasis was on the "Jesus loves" and "precious in His sight" parts. But we still meant it, all of it.

In the context of the kind of afternoon I was having, I saw the wisdom of child's play and the songs that go with it. How many problems of this world could be solved if we could just catch a glimpse of the idea that all people are precious in His sight? How many people suffer every day because we don't realize or care that God loves His children in the world? How many times have we been caught in a situation where we just wanted to shout out, "God made us different by design, but He still loves us"?

We develop political systems and idealogies; we build nations and empires; we direct programs and policies all in order to achieve the reality of the words of a Sunday School song.

That afternoon, I listened to arguments. I interpreted, moderated, mediated, exchanged, translated, and organized. I structured compromises, constructed scenarios, and developed strategies of procedure. But I did all that because I'm not much of a teacher. If I had had the natural teaching gift of Mrs. Smith, I would have found some crayons and some old leftover wallpaper, and I would have taught those people to sing,

> Jesus loves the little children,
> All the children of the world.
> Red and yellow, black and white,
> They are precious in His sight,
> Jesus loves the little children of the world.

If it would have had the same effect on the people at that meeting that Mrs. Smith's song had on me, it would have been more valuable than our arguments and strategies.

The Lesson of
GIVING AN ANSWER

BOBBY MACK PALMER was a strange fellow. We called him strange because he was different from the rest of us. But maybe we were the strange ones and he was normal.

In those days we wouldn't have known what the word "shy" meant, but Bobby Mack was the kind of kid who had to leave the classroom to blow his nose.

Bobby Mack didn't talk much, but he wasn't really quiet. He made noises. In other words, Bobby Mack was the Sunday School Class Special Effects Man.

When we studied the Children of Israel wandering in the wilderness, he sat in his chair staring at Mrs. Murphy, not answering questions, but going,

179

"Klopt—Klopt—Klopt." When we told him he didn't sound like a horse, he explained that those were camels walking in the sand.

When we studied about the shepherds of the Bible, and there were a lot of them, he would make the sounds of sheep baaing.

When we studied about how God made the water burn, he made the sound of a fire truck.

But the strangest thing he ever did was on the morning that our lesson leaflet was labeled, "Exodus 28:1-14—Priestly Garments."

Mrs. Murphy picked Bobby Mack to read first, and we listened attentively, not so much because we were interested in what the Word said, but because we were eager to hear what Bobby Mack might add.

He started, "And take thou unto thee Aaron thy brother and his sons with him from among the Children of Israel, that he may minister unto Me in the priest's office, even Aaron . . . , even Aaron . . . , even Aar . . . ," and he paused before he came to Nadab, Abihu, Eleazar, and Ithamar and he got that look on his face that you might get if your father caught you riding the calves out behind the barn. Then he jumped up and ran across the room and crawled under the little table by the door. And no amount of coaxing by Mrs. Murphy or teasing by us could call him out again.

As we walked out the door, Mrs. Murphy said, "Bobby Mack, come out from under that table. Always be prepared to give an answer to everyone who asks you to give the reason for the hope that you have." And Bobby Mack followed us to church.

Pronouncing hard words out loud is always a challenging and demoralizing task even for the boldest. But pronouncing hard Bible words out loud is an especially excruciating endeavor. If you mispronounce them, everybody looks at you as if you're not a good Christian. And they look as though you ought to pray that God won't punish you because you can't say Nadab, Abihu, Eleazar, and Ithamar— the sons of Aaron—or even Jehoiachin. Besides that, regardless of how you say the names, someone will tell you that you said them wrong.

Nevertheless, hiding under the table did seem to be a bit bizarre at the time. But as the years have gone by, and I've had time to reflect on Bobby Mack's behavior as if it were a parable, I've come to realize that I might have been too harsh.

That's a fairly common human response to diffi-cult passages and times. Sometimes I go to great lengths to avoid the people with whom I think I have had a conflict. There have been days when I have retreated into the bathroom to wash my hands fifty times to avoid meeting a colleague. Sometimes I go to great lengths to avoid telling people who don't know me well the most impor-tant fact about me.

Not long ago I was speaking to a "secular" group, whoever "secular" people are. It was a large group of about a thousand. When I had fin-ished, someone up near the front asked, so that everybody could hear, "How did you learn to be such an optimist?"

As I stood there in front of those one thousand "secular" people, my first impulse was to run hide under the table like Bobby Mack had done, but I remembered the instruction of the Lord through the mouth of Mrs. Murphy, and I boldly gave an answer or reason for the hope that is within me.

That's what I learned in Sunday School and that's all I really need to know.

The Lesson of
COTTON CHOPPING

SOMETIMES YOU CAN LEARN the lessons of Sunday School even when you're not there.

One day in the beauty of early June, I was chopping cotton. Now, chopping cotton is a rather important activity in the overall theme of feeding and clothing the nation, but it is also an activity fraught with unexcitement. In other words, you walk through the red dust all day and cut weeds away from the cotton plants.

In our high tech era, cotton choppers often minimize the tedium by wearing miniature tape players and headsets. But in the pregadget age, we resorted to other means. For example, if there were several workers in the same field, we could walk alongside a married couple and eavesdrop on their quarreling. That's what I was doing on the day I learned so much.

In the middle of the afternoon, the woman said to the man, "Would you come over in my row and help me cut these big weeds?"

"Dear," the man replied rather good naturedly, "remember what the Bible says, 'God helps those who help themselves.' "

"The Bible doesn't say that," the woman answered curtly. "You're just lazy."

"Does too," the man answered. "I went to Sunday School more than you did when I was a kid. I should know what the Bible says."

"Well, it doesn't say anything like that," the woman responded. And with that vigorous beginning, the argument raged for a full thirty minutes.

Finally, either realizing that he didn't have a case or weary from the debate, the man conceded, but only just a bit. "Well, maybe the Bible doesn't say that. But at least that's what my Sunday School teacher told us."

In this simple cotton field testimony, there seems to be a rather profound message. Some thirty years later, the man remembered the words of his teacher and still thought it was the Gospel. That's both a promise and a reprimand.

The Lesson of
THE SWEETER DAY

THE GOOD THING about learning songs in Sunday School is that for the rest of your life, they take on the look of the person that you first heard sing them.

I'm sure that you have heard some variation of this little assumption so often that surely you have a defense against it. Someone is always seeing similarities where none exist. The old adage tells us that dogs look like their masters, but I don't believe that. Of course, I only know two dog owners. About the biggest person I know owns a Chihuahua and about the smallest person I know owns a St. Bernard. There's another adage that tells us that cars look like their owners, but about the only people I know who really put much stock in that are teenage girls.

I agree that seeing these kinds of similarities stretches the imagination a bit, but I still maintain that songs can look like the people who sing them. Of course, this isn't true with all songs or all singers. Some songs just seem to be tailor-made for specific people. How often have you heard someone sing a song, and you say to yourself, "That fits"? From then on, anyone else who attempts to sing that song won't quite make it. On the other hand, how often do you see someone who attempts to sing a song that doesn't quite fit?

During opening exercises, Mrs. Henderson didn't sing too much. Mrs. Smith always led, and Mrs. Henderson sat out among the children herding, corralling, and coaxing. But on special days when we sang one special song, Mrs. Smith would step aside for Mrs. Henderson to come up and lead.

And that was so right. It was Mrs. Henderson's song, and everybody knew it. She's the one who taught it to us. She's the one who led us and corrected us if we didn't understand. And she's the one who knew what it meant.

Every day with Jesus
　is sweeter than the day before,
Every day with Jesus
　I love Him more and more,
Jesus saves and keeps me,
　and He's the one I'm waiting for,
Every day with Jesus
　is sweeter than the day before.

As she would lead by singing above us from her place in the front, even the restless and the perpetual mischievous would cease their wiggling and gouging and stand still with calmness in body and soul; and the room was filled with a certain quiet, a serene and peaceful kind of quiet rather than a forced or manipulated quiet.

Although "hearty" was the descriptive word for most of our singing, "peaceful" would be appropriate to describe how we participated when Mrs. Henderson sang.

As she would lead by singing above us, we didn't hear the age in her voice or see the trembling in her hands. With our heads partially bowed in a reverence required by the moment, we watched and followed and said to ourselves, "This is so right."

This was Mrs. Henderson's song because it was her life. Mrs. Henderson was everybody's grandmother. She was the kind of lady we all thought we knew better than we really did. The reason for that was not deception but a special kind of caring. We children talked to Mrs. Henderson more than we talked to any other adult in church; and because of that, we thought we knew her; but in reality, in those conversations we talked and she listened.

Frequently she would carry things in the pocket of her dress and would surprise us with some little special gift—a cookie, a special piece of embroidery, or something she carved from a piece of twig. But these gifts were conceived and designed for the specific individual, and a gift from Mrs. Henderson became a prized possession, something that we cherished because it reminded us that some adult really had thought about us.

Mrs. Henderson knew Jesus personally. She was on a first-name basis with Him. She prayed often and long. She read her Bible thoroughly and deeply, and she waited with great excitement for that day that Jesus would come again.

She was the only Christian I have ever known who spent more time celebrating Easter than celebrating Christmas. She baked special goodies, mailed out announcement cards, and gave us gifts.

Each year we had a children's Christmas play to satisfy the needs of the rest of the church, but we had an Easter play to satisfy Mrs. Henderson.

And each day with Mrs. Henderson was sweeter than the day before because each day she learned to love Jesus more. For her, true excitement was learning something new about Jesus. The Bible was a gold mine of rich nuggets contributing to the plentiful life, and every day she dug and dug until she found that special nugget for the day so that she could love Jesus more. On Sunday, she would describe those nuggets to us with such vividness that we learned to love Him more too.

One day in early June when the sky was luscious and the valley was alive with plants and it was early enough in the summer vacation that we hadn't grown bored yet, I went down to Mrs. Henderson's house to help her hoe her garden.

During the afternoon, we worked together and we talked. Or rather I talked and Mrs. Henderson listened and asked, and I talked more. But then in what seemed to be a moment out of context, she said that it would thrill her if I would sing her a song. I winced and explained to Mrs. Henderson my sore rib syndrome and that my nickname was Off-Key Cliff. She smiled a smile of reassurance instead of ridicule, and told me that she had a song just for me. She would teach it to me and it would be my special song for the rest of my life. I was excited about that possibility, and she was so convincing that for a moment, I actually believed I could do it. I listened, and she sang — the only song I had ever heard her sing.

> Every day with Jesus
> is sweeter than the day before,
> Every day with Jesus
> I love Him more and more,
> Jesus saves and keeps me,
> and He's the one I'm waiting for,
> Every day with Jesus
> is sweeter than the day before.

When she finished, she pleaded with me to try, but she pleaded with such gentleness and genuineness that I could attempt it without any hint of fear that I might be off key or any hint of the feeling of disloyalty that I had taken her song.

I sang and it felt good. Since my ears are on the side instead of the front, I can't hear myself sing, so I don't know whether it sounded good or not. But it felt good.

When I had finished, Mrs. Henderson had moisture in her eyes and she told me that I had done it beautifully. Then she told me that I should sing that song because it was the song that fit me. And since I believe that songs can fit the people who sing them, and because I had seen her sing the song, I believed her. And I have sung that song every day since. I don't sing out loud nor in crowds. I probably don't even sing on key.

I don't know whether the song fits my voice or not, but I pray that it fits my life the way it fit Mrs. Henderson.

The Lesson of
THE URGENT CHILDREN

WHEN YOU SEE THE WORLD through the eyes of a child, you get one perspective. As you grow older, you get another. There are some who might argue that this is the difference between perception and reality — and that one perspective is more valid than the other. But I don't agree. It seems to me that we need both perspectives; as they combine, they give us a clearer sense of the whole of life.

Now that I'm an adult, I have begun to see new meaning in some of those childhood Sunday School experiences. There is a reason why you sing before you study. There is a reason why one person prays long and the other short. There is a reason why the little children are in the back room.

After having spent terms of service as a teacher in the adult Sunday School department, I have even learned a new function for children. They remind us when to change activities and get serious.

In the church I now attend, the adult class meets upstairs in a room with big windows where the bright Sunday sun floods in and warms our faces and hearts. We have cushioned comfortable chairs and the carpet is thick. In this environment and with these people, Sunday School is a pleasant place to be. Through the week, I find myself looking forward to the warmth of Sunday morning.

The children meet in the back room of the basement. They don't have big windows, and they don't have cushioned chairs or carpet. But they do have a bell which tells them when to start and when to finish.

Upstairs we don't have a bell. We don't even have a clock. But we don't need it. We have something even more dependable to tell us when class is over—the children. Regardless of the depth of our discussion, regardless of the sincerity of the moment, the adult class ends when the bell rings downstairs and the children come running up armed with smiles on their faces, stored-up energy in their limbs, and today's artwork in their hands. When they come bouncing into the room, we know that class is over and it is time to commence learning in a more serious vein.

It isn't just their presence that interrupts, even when they manage to restrain themselves from barging in or banging on the door. These children interrupt because they bring a new level of energy and urgency into the place. The artwork is more than crayon marks on paper. It always comes with a story, and the story is urgent. It must be retold and retold right now.

Some people, and particularly some adult teachers, might find that kind of terminus to a good session somewhat disconcerting. But I don't. In fact, I'm not sure but what it's scriptural.

One day Jesus was holding services. The disciples were on usher duty. When the children came barging in with their stories to tell, the disciples, being the good ushers that they were, said something like, "Shh. You'll have to wait quietly out here in the hall. Jesus is talking seriously about the kingdom."

But that wasn't what Jesus wanted. He said, "Wait a minute. You people have it all wrong. These children are the ones who know about the kingdom. If we don't learn from them, we won't know how to enter it. Let those children come to me, and let's all get serious about this business of learning how to be children of God."

In our class, we follow that little piece of advice every Sunday morning, exactly at ten minutes until eleven. And I know the time even without a clock or bell.

The Lesson of
THE GOOD NEIGHBOR

HOW LONG HAD IT BEEN? Twenty years? Five years? Fourteen years? Six weeks? In my remembering the chronology had been scrambled, and the people and experiences ran together and around each other, jumping into my consciousness in no order or sequence!

But I was going back for Rally Day. Although no one knew it at the time, this would be the last Rally Day ever. This little country congregation, like so many others, was becoming a victim of progress. As more powerful tractors were produced, as farms grew larger and families were more scattered, the children, the people of the next generation, left the valley for careers and fame elsewhere. Eventually the congregation was so small that maintaining a church was not considered sound stewardship.

But this was Rally Day, and there would be a crowd—a crowd of the present but an even bigger crowd of the past and the memories. I was going back. There are those who say you can't go home again, but I've never quite figured out what that means. I go home quite regularly in my memories.

Not only was I going back, but I was taking a crowd—my new loved ones. This was the exciting part. The loved ones and the legends of our youth are an integral part of who we are now, for they have made us and shaped us into what we are and are becoming.

Through the years we adopt and are adopted by our new loved ones—spouses and children.

As they come into our lives *in medias res,* we struggle to find the memories and the words to recount that which has shaped us. Because of our inadequacies with language, we long for the day when we can go back, when the new loved ones can meet the old loved ones and can visualize what was and then believe the legends and the happenings.

The day for joining the past and the present had come. Now my wife and children could put faces to names and curtain walls to places and corners.

Although this was Sunday School, I was going mainly because of the memories — for the reliving and the reunion. It wasn't that I was calloused or too sophisticated to learn; but I had been through it so many years at this place, and so many years at other places so like this place, and I had been through it all in my memories over and over again. I was so focused on the past that I forgot that I might learn something to be used in the future.

I wasn't disappointed. The place was as royal as I had remembered, but smaller. The people were as gracious, and I winced in mock embarrassment when they told my children how I had acted in Sunday School when I was their age.

And the ritual was just as rich. Because there were only a few children, my own and the children of my peers were called up to recite what Bible verses they might know, and we nodded with the joy of tradition when several recited John 3:16. And we laughed out loud with the reality of tradition when some recited, "Jesus wept."

And we all sang the old choruses including "Every day with Jesus," and I worshiped on the predicate.

The Sword Drill was just as fast as it used to be, and the winner licked her fingers just as I remembered Mary Alice doing.

As the ceremony progressed, and I regressed to being a little boy again, I punched my family members at the regular intervals with that knowing punch that says, "See! See what I told you! Now do you believe me?" Or I punched sometimes just to remind them that I already knew what was coming next.

For I did know what was coming next—I had played it all out in my remembering so many times through the years. And now I understood myself a little better—why I hold certain things dear, why I set the objectives I set, and why I read the Bible as I do. There were no surprises—just memories and appreciation.

At the end of the service, the one deacon of memory who was still active in the church stood for the conclusion.

Then I relaxed. The service had been rich. The

memories had been refreshing, but it was now time to return to the present — to get back into the world of now.

In a fashion so typical of many churchgoers, I half listened to the concluding remarks while I put away the hymnal, retrieved the children who had crawled under the pew in front of us, and gathered up belongings strewn by our young family.

After all, concluding remarks are only that — semicolons that lead us from then to now.

But Brother Roy, in a voice made strong through the years of shouting at cattle, and in a spirit made genuine through the years of walking with Jesus, said simply, "Become a Christian. It'll make your neighbor a better person." Then he prayed.

Suddenly that last Rally Day took on an entirely new meaning. I had come for the memories of the old lessons, but I went away with the conviction and the blessing of the new one.

I can only pray that I live my life in such a way that it is easier for my neighbor to be a good person.

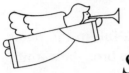

The Lesson of
SUNDAY SCHOOL

THE SNOW WAS BLOWING; the ice was form-
ing; and the curving country roads had already
grown treacherous. We thought of turning back,
but even that seemed dangerous; so we drove on
ahead telling ourselves that it was of no value because surely no one else would venture out on a
morning like this.

Finally, we came over a little hill and spotted
our destination, a small country church sitting
boldly against the climate. Although we had never
been there before, we knew it was the right place.
I had been asked to come to speak, and the directions were clear. But even more importantly, we
knew this was the right place because it looked so
familiar.

To our surprise, the place was full to the point of crowded, and the people inside brought warmth to the church and the day.

After the opening exercise of singing and taking the appropriate offering, the children disappeared behind the closing curtains, and we all began to study.

Standing in front, I tried to get my mouth to speak of adult concerns, but my mind refused and I became a boy again, half expecting The Old Mare to whinny or Mrs. Murphy to call on me to say the books in order. Caught in that tension between past and present, I held class for the requisite period.

When the children came streaming out from behind the curtains and running past me to rejoin their parents in the pews, I knew that class was over, so I moved to a quiet corner where I could reflect.

There I was joined by a man older than I in face and body but, like me, a boy again in memory. He told me of his seventy years in that Sunday School, of the wood stove, and watering tub beneath the tree, of dinner on the grounds, and the Rally Day programs, and of teachers and the Word of God.

He told it all so well that I saw the faces and I heard the words, and I realized that although we had grown up half a country and a generation apart, we were brothers in the Lord and in memory.

Feeling a need to go back to the present but not sure why, I asked him why, after seventy years of being in this Sunday School, he had chosen to risk life and limb to come out on a treacherous morning like this. Surely he had heard all the lessons by now and wasn't expecting anything new.

"Paul told me to come," he told me.

I ran through my mental computer list trying to remember someone named Paul who would have dared recommend me so highly as to bring this man out from his safety.

"Paul?" I asked.

With that he took out a worn Bible. At first I thought it might have been something left over from his boyhood days; but as he began to read, I could tell that it wasn't.

"But as for you, continue in what you have learned and have become convinced of because

207

you know those from whom you learned it; and how from infancy you have known the Holy Scriptures, which are able to make you wise for salvation through faith in Christ Jesus." He closed the Bible, looked at me, and said, "My Sunday School taught me that before I even learned to read."

Praise God for all the Mrs. Smiths, Mrs. Murphys, and Mrs. Hendersons of the world who through the Sunday School have always taught us and are still teaching us all we really need to know.